POCKET
GOOD
GUIDES

GOOD · GUIDES

BEST
LONDON
PUBS &
BARS

GOOD GUIDES

POCKET
GOOD
GUIDES

BEST
LONDON
PUBS &
BARS

Edited by Alisdair Aird
Deputy Editor Fiona Stapley
Assistant Editor Elizabeth Adlington

Associate Editor Robert Unsworth
Managing Editor Karen Fick

Software consultancy Trade Wind Technology

EBURY PRESS

First published in Great Britain in 2004
Ebury Press
Random House
20 Vauxhall Bridge Road
London SW1V 2SA

10 9 8 7 6 5 4 3 2 1

Random House Australia (Pty) Limited
20 Alfred Street, Milsons Point
Sydney
New South Wales 2061, Australia

Random House New Zealand Limited
18 Poland Road, Glenfield, Auckland 10
New Zealand

Random House South Africa (Pty) Limited
Endulini, 5A Jubilee Road
Parktown 2193
South Africa

Random House UK Limited Reg. No. 954009

www.randomhouse.co.uk

A CIP catalogue record for this book is available from the British Library.

ISBN 0 09 189 669X

Papers used by Ebury Press are natural, recyclable products made from wood grown in sustainable forests.

Typeset by Textype, Cambridge
Cover design by Nim Design
Front cover image © Jane Glasson
Printed and bound in Denmark by Nørhaven A/S, Viborg

Introduction

The best of London's pubs and bars

This new book is an offshoot from our best-selling annual *Good Pub Guide*, the byword in honest independent reporting on Britain's best pubs for over 20 years. The Good Guides team have used their unrivalled inspection expertise and confidential reports from their army of in-the-know informants to track down London's best pubs and bars. From relaxed riverside haunts to charming little-known hideaways, from jazz and theatre pubs to stylish cocktail bars, from candlelit cellars to celebrity hotspots, we have hand-picked a galaxy of places that you'll be delighted to discover.

Very good food can now be had in London bars and pubs – we tell you just where to find it. And we include places with exceptional beers and wines, and with particularly tempting cocktails. A special chapter covers London's top hotel bars, with detailed descriptions right down to the nitty-gritty directions that let you walk straight in, knowing exactly where you are heading for.

To contact the Pocket Good Guides team,
please write to

Pocket Good Guides
Freepost TN1 569
Wadhurst
E. Sussex
TN5 7BR

or check out
www.goodguides.co.uk

Contents

Using the Guide

All the large print entries in this book have been inspected anonymously by the editorial team of *The Good Pub Guide* – the authoritative annual guide to Britain's best pubs for more than 20 years. Prices, opening times and other factual details have been checked with the pubs and bars themselves.

We also have nearly 2,000 current reports from readers on London pubs and bars. The small print entries are based primarily on their recommendations, though we have also inspected nearly 100 of these, including virtually all the bars listed.

Entries are listed in order of area, starting with Central London (EC areas followed by SW1 and other SW areas, then W1, W2, then WC1 & WC2), then North, South, West and East. In each area, pubs are grouped alphabetically under each postal district in turn, main entries first, then small print entries in that district. The entries are numbered consecutively, and these numbers are shown on the maps.

At the end, we include a chapter on London's top hotel bars – an interesting change from other bars, often rather special.

In the directions, the ⊖ symbol shows the nearest tube station to each bar or pub; ⇌ shows the nearest rail station if there is no tube handy; DLR stands for Docklands Light Railway.

We note days when main entry pubs have told us they don't do food or are closed altogether, and when we know that small print ones are. You should play safe at weekends, particularly in the City, and check first with any pub before planning an expedition that depends on getting a meal there. Many City pubs may close fairly early in the evening.

We show bedroom prices for those rare places which have them. If we give just one price, it is the total price including breakfast for two people sharing a double or twin-bedded room for one night. Otherwise, prices before the / are for single occupancy, prices after it for double. A capital B against the price means that it includes a private bathroom, a capital S a private shower. If there's a choice of rooms at different prices, we normally give the cheapest. If there are seasonal price variations, we give the summer price (the highest).

We rely heavily on the many readers who are kind enough to send us reports, describing places they think should be added to the *Guide*, and commenting on existing entries; and please tell us of any disappointments, or changes (London pubs and bars can change dramatic-ally overnight). Write to Pocket Good Guides, FREEPOST TN1 569, WADHURST, E. Sussex TN5 7BR (no stamp needed), or use our web site www.goodguides.co.uk.

CENTRAL LONDON

1. BISHOPS FINGER
West Smithfield, EC1; opposite Bart's Hospital; ⊖ Farringdon
There are few places in London where you'll find Shepherd
Neame beers as well kept as at this swish little pub, in a
verdant square beside Smithfield Market. Comfortable and
smartly civilised, the well laid-out room has bright yellow
walls, big windows, elegant tables with fresh flowers on the
polished bare boards, a few pillars, and comfortably
cushioned chairs under one wall lined with framed prints.
Shepherd Neame Bitter, Spitfire, Bishops Finger and
seasonal brews on handpump, with a wide choice of wines
(eight by the glass), ten malt whiskies, and several ports and
champagnes; friendly service. Good lunchtime food from an
open kitchen beside the bar includes tasty ciabatta
sandwiches filled with things like goats cheese, pesto and
beef tomato (from £3.35), home-made burgers in focaccia
bread (£5.95), a dozen or so types of sausage with mash
(from £6.75; they come from a speciality shop nearby), and
on Thursday and Friday beer-battered cod and hand-cut
chips (£6.95). There are a couple of tables outside.
*Bar food (12-3) ~ (020) 7248 2341 ~ Children welcome ~
Open 11-11; cl Sat and Sun, bank hols*

2. CELLAR GASCON

West Smithfield, EC1; ⊖ Farringdon

This civilised french-style city bar has an unusual but mouth-watering selection of wines from Gascony – a temptation hard to resist for the suited businessmen who congregate here. They do range further afield, including, for example, 23 champagnes. The narrow room has a single row of brown leather scoop bar stools and window banquettes flanking varnished wooden-topped tables on a little raised platform to the left, with more stools along the welcoming bar counter. Up a few steps at the back a little lounge area has blue leather scoop swivel stools around a couple of low tables. The décor is predominantly grey and dark brown, with chocolate leather panels softening the exposed brickwork, a blue and purple map of Gascony brightening one wall, and spotlights and cone-shaped hanging lamps. One shelf holds a few books and magazines, but the prime reading matter is the leather-bound menu with its tempting selection of french tapas-style food – it even includes a choice of seven different types of foie gras. More than 30 dishes include various kinds of pâté (from £2.80), smoked eel and leek terrine (£3.50), seven different types of foie gras (from £4), salmon mousse (£4.50), popular warm Gascony pie (£5), scallops (£5.75) and confit of fennel and bass (£6). They also do a two-course lunch (£9.50). The service is good, and the piped music is unobtrusive.

Bar food (all day) ~ Restaurant ~ (020) 7796 0600 ~

*Children allowed (but may be a bit smoky) ~ Open 12-12;
cl wknds, also bank hols and two wks over Christmas*

3. EAGLE
**Farringdon Road, EC1; opposite Bowling Green Lane car
park; ⊖ Farringdon or Old Street**
Still packing them in with an excellent and distinctive choice
of mediterranean-style meals that rank among the capital's
very best, this was the original London gastro-pub. It buzzes
with life, and despite the emphasis on eating, always feels
chatty and pubby. And though it's often very busy, the
atmosphere is so relaxed that readers who've popped in
intending to have just a drink find it hard to resist the aromas
from the open kitchen. Made with the finest ingredients,
typical dishes might include celeriac, ham and potato soup
(£5), tuscan bean and bread stew with cavolo nero or
spaghetti with asparagus, truffle oil and parmesan cheese
(£8), marinated rump steak sandwich (£9), cuttlefish braised
with peas, wine and garlic on bruschetta (£10.50), lamb leg
chop, roast carrots and jerusalem artichokes with watercress
salad (£11), and poached wild sea trout, rocket, french
beans and horseradish (£12); they also do unusual spanish,
sardinian or goats milk cheeses (£6.50), and portuguese
custard tarts (£1); they now take credit cards. On weekday
lunchtimes especially, dishes from the blackboard menu can
run out or change fairly quickly, so it really is worth getting
here as early as you possibly can if you're hoping to eat.

Furnishings in the single room are simple but stylish – school chairs, a random assortment of tables, a couple of sofas on bare boards, and modern paintings on the walls (there's an art gallery upstairs, with direct access from the bar). Quite a mix of customers, but it's fair to say there's a proliferation of young media folk (*The Guardian* is based just up the road). It gets particularly busy in the evening (and can occasionally be slightly smoky then), so isn't the sort of place you'd go for a quiet dinner, or a smart night out. Well kept Charles Wells Eagle and Bombardier on handpump, good wines including a dozen by the glass, good coffee, and properly made cocktails; piped music (sometimes loud). There are times during the week when the Eagle's success means you may have to wait for a table, or at least not be shy about sharing; it can be quieter at weekends.

Bar food (12.30-2.30(3.30 Sat and Sun); 6.30-10.30) ~ Restaurant ~ No credit cards ~ (020) 7837 1353 ~ Children welcome ~ Dogs allowed in bar ~ Open 12-11 (5 Sun); cl Sun evening, bank hols

4. JERUSALEM TAVERN

Britton Street, EC1; ⊖ Farringdon

There's plenty to recommend at this carefully restored old coffee house, now one of London's very best pubs, but the highlight is undoubtedly the collection of delicious St Peters beers. It's one of only a few pubs belonging to the small, Suffolk-based brewery, and stocks pretty much their full range. Half a dozen are tapped from casks behind the little bar counter: depending on the season you'll find St Peters Best, Fruit Beer, Golden Ale, Grapefruit, Strong, Porter, Wheat Beer, Winter, and Spiced Ales. The rest are usually available in their elegant, distinctively shaped bottles (you may already have come across these in supermarkets); if you develop a taste for them – and they are rather addictive – they sell them to take away. The pub is a vivid re-creation of a dark 18th-c tavern, seeming so genuinely old that you'd never guess the work was done only a few years ago. The current building was developed around 1720, originally as a merchant's house, then becoming a clock and watchmaker's. It still has the shop front added in 1810, immediately behind which is a light little room with a couple of wooden tables and benches, a stack of *Country Life* magazines, and some remarkable old tiles on the walls at either side. This leads to the tiny dimly lit bar, which has a couple of unpretentious tables on the bare boards, and another up some stairs on a discreetly precarious-feeling though perfectly secure balcony. A plainer back room has a few more tables, as well as a fireplace, and a stuffed fox in a case. There's a relaxed, chatty feel in the evenings – though as the pub becomes better-known it's getting harder to bag a seat here then, and it can feel crowded at times. Blackboards list the simple but well liked lunchtime food: soup, good big sandwiches in various breads (from £4.50), and a couple of changing hot dishes such as bangers and mash (£6.50) or lamb shank

(£7.50). Prompt, friendly service. A couple of tables outside overlook the quiet street, though take care if standing out here: some readers have found that a neighbouring property's anti-vandalism paint has left a lasting impression on their bags. Note: the pub no longer opens at weekends.
Bar food (12-3; not evenings) ~ (020) 7490 4281 ~
Children welcome ~ Dogs allowed in bar ~ Open 11-11

5. OLDE MITRE
Ely Place, EC1; the easiest way to find it is from the narrow passageway beside 8 Hatton Garden; ⊖ Chancery Lane
Nothing seems to change at this carefully rebuilt old tavern, a delightful hidden treasure standing out for its distinctive character and history, and exceptional welcome and service. Unless you approach it from Hatton Garden it can be notoriously difficult to find, but it more than repays the effort; the landlord clearly loves his job, and works hard to pass that enjoyment on to his customers. The cosy dark-panelled small rooms have antique settles and – particularly in the back room, where there are more seats – old local pictures and so forth. It gets good-naturedly packed between 12.30 and 2.15, filling up again in the early evening, but in the early afternoons and by around nine becomes a good deal more tranquil. An upstairs room, mainly used for functions, may double as an overflow at peak periods. Well kept Adnams, Ind Coope Burton and Tetleys on handpump; notably chatty staff. No music, TV or machines – the only game here is

darts. Served all day, bar snacks are limited to scotch eggs or pork pies (£1), and really good value toasted sandwiches with cheese, ham, pickle or tomato (£1.75). There are some pot plants and jasmine in the narrow yard between the pub and St Ethelreda's church. Note: the pub doesn't open weekends. The iron gates that guard one entrance to Ely Place are a reminder of the days when the law in this district was administered by the Bishops of Ely.
*Bar food (11-9.15) ~ (020) 7405 4751 ~ Open 11-11;
cl wknds, bank hols*

6. BETSEY TROTWOOD
Farringdon Rd; ⊖ Farringdon
Tidy and efficient local for *Guardian* newspaper and other nearby offices, Shepherd Neame ales, friendly staff

7. BLEEDING HEART
Bleeding Heart Yard, off Greville St; ⊖ Farringdon
Striking blood-red building, with a café-style atmosphere in the airy one-room bar, and an emphasis on good french-style food (they open for breakfast from 7am); scrubbed floorboards, a mix of wooden café tables and chairs, big windows on two sides (half-covered with information about the tavern's history), pale mustard walls, red ceiling, brick fireplace and fresh flowers; wooden banisters and a glass screen etched with a street map of the area separate the bar from stairs leading down to the formal restaurant (with an open kitchen); smartly dressed staff, Adnams Bitter, Broadside and Fisherman from the ornate mahogany-and-mirrors bar, also Bitburger Pils and a good imaginative selection of wines by the glass; cl wknds

8. CLERKENWELL HOUSE
Hatton Wall; ⊖ Farringdon

Relaxed warehouse-style bar, divided into different areas by an eclectic mix of comfortably scuffed 70s leather settees and swivel chairs, and orange pillars; mostly whitewashed walls, though one with maroon and turquoise panels has modern artwork for sale, some brown 70s wallpaper, spotlighting, and well trampled floorboards; DJ box and little kitchen either end of the bar, which is brightened up by crimson panels; mostly mediterranean-style food, the usual lagers and so forth, relaxed service; a wrought-iron spiral staircase with a gilded female statue leads down to the basement pool room (£6 an hour, £10 deposit); popular with a young crowd, with piped music, DJs and live music nights; open 12(Sat 6)-11

9. MASQUE HAUNT
Old St/Bunhill Row; ⊖ Moorgate

Impressive long Wetherspoons with some alcoves in the open-plan back no smoking area, lots of books in raised section; their usual food all day, efficient friendly staff, eight well kept ales most from small breweries; open all day

10. O'HANLONS
Tysoe St; ⊖ Angel or Farringdon

Friendly traditional local, bare boards and yellow paintwork, tasty beers from O'Hanlons in Devon, also Brakspears and Fullers London Pride, enjoyable home-made food from baguettes to a few reasonably priced daily specials and usually Sun lunch, with good irish stew in winter; irish folk night Thurs; a couple of tables outside; open all day

11. OLD RED LION
St John St; ⊖ Farringdon
Theatre bar, simple and atmospherically dark; well kept Adnams Broadside

12. POTEMKIN
Clerkenwell Rd; ⊖ Farringdon
Gracefully curved little russian bar, with huge windows, light wooden tables on walnut-coloured floorboards, with a mix of padded brown leather chairs and banquettes, and coffee-coloured leather cubes; deep blue walls, one with softly lit alcoves, mirrors, a couple of pictures, spotlighting, and elegant flowers; an awesome selection of vodkas draws the crowds (from honey and pepper to tarragon or thai fruits), rare georgian wines and bottled beers; quite an emphasis on the good russian food inc delicious borscht and sturgeon, efficient service from the russian staff, piped russian music; a dazzling mirrored corridor leads down to a formal basement restaurant

13. RISING SUN
Cloth Fair; ⊖ Barbican
Lofty linked bars in muted browns, with elaborate carved dark woodwork, some nice frosted glass, ornate bookcase, lots of little tables, stools and benches around the edges, relaxed atmosphere, friendly staff, well kept Sam Smiths, good value food from baguettes to Sun lunch; views of church; chess, dominoes, cribbage, upstairs lounge (not always open) up steep stairs; fruit machine, may be piped music

14. SEKFORDE ARMS
Sekforde St; ⊖ Farringdon
Small and comfortably simple corner Youngs local with friendly
licensees, well kept beers and wide range of well priced straightforward food, with nice pictures inc Spy caricatures, upstairs
restaurant; pavement tables

EC2 (City/Bank/Shoreditch)

15. CANTALOUPE
Charlotte Road, EC2; ⊖ Old Street
One of the first of the new wave of Shoreditch bars and still a
front-runner, this lively dim-lit place has a strongly post-
industrial décor in its front main room, with massive rough
tables and backless benches on huge wooden flooring
panels, plain big-windowed walls, sturdy school radiators,
and silvery ducting snaking among the black ceiling's fans.
There is plenty of standing room, and at night when the big
speaker system, throttled down by day, really gets going, the
place gets packed – and loud. The long neat bar counter is
inviting, with no bar stools but a good footrail, and a
tempting drinks choice including Charles Wells Banana
Bread beer (it really does taste of that), a dozen or so well
priced wines by the glass, and lots of coffees. From the open
kitchen comes a wide range of enterprising bar food
including tapas such as fried spinach and chickpeas with
cumin and garlic (£2.50) or chargrilled periperi pork (£4),

toasted focaccia with tuna, olives, egg, tomato and green beans (£4), nachos (£4.50), lamb burger with hummus, aubergine and rocket (£7), and generous sharing platters (from £10). Beyond the kitchen is a comfortable inner room with leather settees and wing armchairs, and greenery climbing along its red walls and ceiling, and past that a further bar area with rather elegant, spindly, modernist stools and tall tables, and a serving counter with appealing yellow backlighting. There is also a restaurant with banquettes in bays. Good disabled access and facilities.

Bar food (all day) ~ (020) 7729 5566 ~ Children allowed till 5 ~ Open 11-12; 12-11.30 Sun; cl some bank hols inc 25 Dec and 1 Jan

16. FOX

Paul Street, EC2; ⊖ Old Street

Wandering into the bare-boards downstairs bar here for the first time, you could be forgiven for assuming it's no more than a basic London boozer, but don't be fooled: the Fox has the same landlord as the Eagle (*see* entry 3), and a similar emphasis on excellent food. Unpretentious yet relaxed and comfortable, it has lots of stools around a central servery, and small round tables and well worn furnishings under a dark red ceiling; the first clues that this is something rather unusual are the laid-back jazz and a chalkboard listing the excellent range of well chosen wines (a dozen by the glass). Well kept Charles Wells Bombardier on handpump, and unusual lunchtime bar snacks such as a good hot salt beef sandwich (£5.50), ploughman's with caerphilly, or watermelon with goats curd (both £6). A staircase leads up to the smarter dining room, with its big refectory-style table down the middle, and a very appealing canopied terrace. This is ostensibly the place to enjoy the full menu, though you can have it down in the bar as well. A typical choice might include starters like vichyssoise or serrano ham with broad beans, main courses such as semolina gnocchi, roast tomatoes and rocket, wild salmon and samphire, or neck of lamb and champ, and puddings such as peach and raspberry pavlova or lemon and polenta cake; two courses are £15.50, three courses £19. Service up here is friendly and helpful; they take credit cards. The Fox perhaps takes a bit more effort to seek out than the Eagle, and it will be interesting to see if it causes the same stir.

Bar food (12-3 Mon-Fri) ~ Restaurant ~ (020) 7729 5708 ~ Dogs welcome ~ Open 12-11; cl wknds

17. CORNEY & BARROW
Old Broad St; ⊖ Bank

The exceptional range of wines by two glass sizes (including reasonably priced house wines) is the big draw at this small chain of London bars, run by a long-established wine merchant – they do a special champagne offer on your birthday; this bar is a good example, long and rather narrow, with efficient staff at the very long counter, sparse modern décor (here polished limestone and lots of opaque glass make for such lively acoustics that two dozen people can sound like 100 conversations – folk do talk rather a lot in this part of London), tall brown-cushioned chairs and stools at high wood or granite tables or along glass elbow-shelves, plenty of standing room; good coffee, breakfasts, modern lunches and evening snacks, well stored cigars; piped music and high silenced TVs; open all day from 7.30am, cl wknds

18. DIRTY DICKS
Bishopsgate; ⊖/≥ Liverpool Street
Re-creation of traditional City tavern with barrel tables in bare-boards bar, interesting old prints inc one of Nathaniel Bentley, the original Dirty Dick; Youngs full beer range kept well, decent food inc open sandwiches, baguettes and reasonably priced hot dishes, pleasant service, cellar wine bar with wine racks overhead in brick barrel-vaulted ceiling; loads of character – fun for foreign visitors

19. HAMILTON HALL
Bishopsgate; ⊖/≥ Liverpool Street, also entrance from station
Big busy Wetherspoons pub, flamboyant Victorian baroque décor, plaster nudes and fruit mouldings, chandeliers, mirrors, upper mezzanine, good-sized upstairs no smoking section (can get crowded and smoky downstairs), comfortable groups of seats; reliable food all day from well filled sandwiches up, interesting changing well kept real ales, decent wines, good prices; silenced machines, no piped music; tables outside; open all day

20. JAMIES
Gresham St; ⊖ Bank
One of a small chain, this has a cosier and more intimate atmosphere than many London bars; not large, it has standing space by the long marble-topped entrance bar, with bar stools facing

alcoved mirrors opposite and along a heavy mahogany back balustrade, and nightlights along ledges; the back part is carpeted, with big polo paintings above the tables; friendly antipodean staff, particularly good, usefully described range of wines by the glass, modern food from sandwiches up, discreet downstairs lunchtime restaurant, well reproduced up-to-date piped music, open all day; very handy for Guildhall; some of this group's bars are bigger and more lively, with rather less emphasis on wines and more on lagers

21. OLD DR BUTLERS HEAD
Masons Ave; ⊖ Bank
17th-c beamed City pub with more seating than usual, bare boards, dark wood, cream paint, small-paned windows, small tables around big irregularly shaped main room, raised back area with more tables; Shepherd Neame Bitter, Best, Spitfire and Bishops Finger, quick service, lunchtime food, upstairs bar

22. PACIFIC
Bishopsgate; ⊖ Bank
Bright US-style brewpub, not cheap, with beer brewed visibly on the premises, wide choice of food in dining room and upstairs restaurant, good wine choice, friendly often foreign staff

EC3 (City/Monument)

23. GRAND CAFÉ BAR
Royal Exchange, EC3; ⊖ Bank
The imposing, early Victorian, stone-built Royal Exchange, with its magnificent pillared portico, was reworked in 2001

to include two floors of stylish shops, around its spacious roofed courtyard. This bar, run by the Conran group, is on the upper floor, with tables in elegant arched balconies looking down on the concourse below (and overlooking people eating, very publicly, at tables of its smart sister restaurant). The concourse is stone-floored, so a subdued clattery background toing-and-froing drifts up here to the bar, mingling with the piped 1970s pop music – a gentle and rather pleasing contrast of other people's bustle with the relaxed calm of your own comfortable seats at one of the well spaced tables. The furnishings and décor are thoroughly modern – charcoal leather settees, dark maroon or grey leather armchairs, some silvery steel round tables on black pedestals (the balcony ones are dark wood), grey rugs on the woodstrip floor, underlit feature flower arrangements. The bar stools are among the most comfortable we have tried – and the bar itself has a rather decent choice of wines by the glass, including reasonably priced house wines, though it's easy to spend quite a lot more on the good range of tempting cocktails. Good coffee, and plenty of informally black-uniformed young staff. Bar snacks include devilled whitebait (£5.25), creamed scallop ceviche (£9.50) and mixed charcuterie (£10.50), as well as dishes from the downstairs restaurant menu, such as steak and Guinness pie (£13) or toasted lobster sandwich (£15). Note that the lavatories are another floor down, in the basement.

Restaurant ~ (020) 7618 2480 ~ Children in restaurant

(which is open from 8am for breakfast) ~ Open 11–11; cl Sat and Sun, bank hols, around 10 days over Christmas and New Year

24. COCK & WOOLPACK
Finch Lane, off Threadneedle St; ⊖ Bank
Well done modern pastiche of a traditional Victorian pub, more seating than many, inc mirrored central saloon and back snug; well kept Shepherd Neame ales

25. CROSSE KEYS
Gracechurch St; ⊖ Monument
Attractive Wetherspoons in former bank, light and bright with lots of marble, domed ceiling, pillars, ornate wood and plasterwork, panelling, upper gallery; well kept ales inc lots of guest beers from big oval central bar, their usual menu, friendly helpful staff; silenced games machine, no music; no smoking back children's area; open all day but cl 4pm Sat

26. LAMB
Grand Ave, Leadenhall Market; ⊖ Monument
Old-fashioned stand-up bar with spiral stairs to light and airy upper no smoking carpeted lounge bar overlooking market's central crossing; vibrant atmosphere (can get very busy), plenty of tables and corner servery doing good hot carvery rolls, well kept Youngs ales, engraved glass, plenty of ledges and shelves; also basement bar with shiny wall tiling and own entrance

27. SHIP
Talbot Court, off Eastcheap; ⊖ Monument
Quaint bare-boards courtyard pub full of City types, well kept

Adnams, Fullers London Pride and Greene King IPA, lunchtime snacks; a Nicholsons pub

EC4 (City/Fleet Street)

28. BLACK FRIAR
Queen Victoria Street, EC4; ⊖ Blackfriars

This distinctive old favourite now has smart new furniture on its wide forecourt, as well as a new menu with a wider range of food. Of course the main attraction remains its unique décor, which includes some of the best Edwardian bronze and marble art nouveau work to be found anywhere. The inner back room has big bas-relief friezes of jolly monks set into richly coloured florentine marble walls, an opulent marble-pillared inglenook fireplace, a low vaulted mosaic ceiling, gleaming mirrors, seats built into rich golden marble recesses, and tongue-in-cheek verbal embellishments such as 'Silence is Golden' and 'Finery is Foolish'. See if you can spot the opium-smoking hints modelled into the fireplace of the front room. Well kept Adnams, Bass and Fullers London Pride on handpump, and a decent range of wines by the glass; fruit machine. Now served all day, bar food includes sandwiches (from £3.95), pork and herb sausages with mash and onion gravy (£5.75), a vegetarian dish of the day (£5.95), and battered cod and chips or smoked haddock fishcakes (£6.95), Sunday roasts (£6.95). An area around the bar is

no smoking. The pub does get busy, and in the evenings lots of people spill out on to the pavement in front, near the approach to Blackfriars Bridge. If you're coming by tube, choose your exit carefully – it's all too easy to emerge from the network of passageways and find yourself on the wrong side of the street, or marooned on a traffic island.
Bar food (12-9) ~ (020) 7236 5474 ~ Open 11.30-11; 12-11(10.30 Sun) Sat

29. OLD BANK OF ENGLAND

Fleet Street, EC4; ⊖ Temple

From the outside, this rather austere italianate building still looks very much like the subsidiary branch of the Bank of England it once was. But once up the stone steps its spectacular conversion into a pub becomes startlingly clear, and rarely fails to impress first – or even second-time visitors. In the opulent bar, three gleaming chandeliers hang from the exquisitely plastered ceiling high above the unusually tall island bar counter, and the green walls are liberally dotted with old prints, framed bank notes and the like. Though the room is quite spacious, screens between some of the varied seats and tables create a surprisingly intimate feel, and there are several cosier areas at the end, with more seats in a quieter galleried section upstairs. The mural that covers most of the end wall looks like an 18th-c depiction of Justice (one perhaps over-effusive reader compared it with the Sistine Chapel), but in fact features members of the Fuller, Smith and Turner families. Well kept

Fullers Chiswick, ESB, London Pride and seasonal brews on handpump, and around a dozen wines by the glass. Now served all day, good generously served bar food includes soup (£2.75), sandwiches (from £3.50), smoked haddock and salmon fishcakes (£5.75), several pies like leek, mushroom and stilton (£6.25), chicken, red wine and shallot or steak and Fullers Porter (£6.75), pan-fried loch duart salmon (£8.25), and steak (£9.75). The piped music is generally classical or easy listening. It can get busy after work. Note: they don't allow children, and are closed at weekends. In winter the pub is easy to spot by the Olympic-style torches blazing outside. Pies have a long if rather dubious pedigree in this area; it was in the vaults and tunnels below the Old Bank and the surrounding buildings that Sweeney Todd butchered the clients destined to provide the fillings in his mistress Mrs Lovett's nearby pie shop.

Bar food (12-9) ~ Restaurant ~ (020) 7430 2255 ~ Open 11-11; cl wknds, bank hols

30. OLDE CHESHIRE CHEESE

Wine Office Court, off 145 Fleet Street, EC4; ⊖ Blackfriars

The succession of dark, historic little rooms at this atmospheric 17th-c former chop house are a joy to explore, and even though it's one of London's most famous old pubs, it doesn't feel as if it's on the tourist route. Over the years Congreve, Pope, Voltaire, Thackeray, Dickens, Conan Doyle, Yeats and perhaps Dr Johnson have called in, and many

parts appear to have hardly changed since. The unpretentious rooms have bare wooden benches built in to the walls,
sawdust on bare boards, and, on the ground floor, high
beams, crackly old black varnish, Victorian paintings on the
dark brown walls, and big open fires in winter. A particularly
snug room is the tiny one on the right as you enter, but
perhaps the most rewarding bit is the Cellar Bar, down steep
narrow stone steps that look as if they're only going to lead to
the loo, but in fact take you to an unexpected series of cosy
areas with stone walls and ceilings, and some secluded
corners. There's plenty of space, so even though it can get
busy during the week (it's fairly quiet at weekends) it rarely
feels too crowded. Usually served all day, bar food includes
sandwiches or hot paninis, soup, ploughman's (£4.25), and
steak and ale pie, lasagne or various daily specials (£4.75).
Sam Smiths OB on handpump, as usual for this brewery,
extraordinarily well priced (almost £1 less than other beers
can cost at more expensive London pubs); friendly service.
Some of the Cellar Bar is no smoking at lunchtimes.
Bar food (12-9(2 Sun)) ~ Restaurant (Sun) ~
(020) 7353 6170/4388 ~ Children in eating area of
bar and restaurant ~ Open 11-11; 11-3, 5.30-11 Sat; 12-3
Sun; cl Sun evening

31. LONDON STONE
Cannon St; ⊖/⇌ Cannon Street
Gothic basement bar with Hallowe'en feel, wooden booths, cases full of cobwebby potion bottles, skeletons, etc – lavatories in secret compartment hidden behind hinged bookcase; usual drinks and food as well as 'seven deadly sins' cocktails

SW1 (Westminster/Mayfair/Belgravia/Pimlico)

32. ALBERT
Victoria Street, SW1; ⊖ St James's Park
A favourite with the Chelsea pensioners from the Royal Hospital, this bustling 19th-c pub was one of the few buildings in this part of Victoria to escape the Blitz (it's now rather dwarfed by the surrounding faceless cliffs of dark modern glass). There's a wonderfully diverse mix of customers, from tourists and civil servants to even the occasional MP: the division bell is rung to remind them when it's time to get back to Westminster. Always busy – especially on weekday lunchtimes and after work – the huge open-plan bar has a surprisingly airy feel, thanks to great expanses of original, heavily cut and etched windows along three sides, as well as good solid comfortable furniture, an ornate ceiling, and some gleaming mahogany. Service from the big island counter is generally swift and efficient (particularly obliging to people from overseas), with Charles Wells Bombardier, Courage Best and Directors, Fullers London Pride and

Greene King Abbot, and sometimes a more unusual guest on handpump. The separate food servery is good value, offering sandwiches (from £2.75), salads (from £4) and several hearty home-cooked hot dishes such as turkey casserole, fish and chips, sweet and sour chicken and vegetable lasagne (all £5.50); usefully, there's something available all day. The upstairs restaurant does an eat-as-much-as-you-like carvery, better than average (all day inc Sunday, £16.50 for three courses and coffee); it may be worth booking ahead. The handsome staircase that leads up to it is lined with portraits of former Prime Ministers. The back bar is no smoking. Sometimes loudish piped music, fruit machine. Handily placed between Victoria and Westminster, the pub is one of the great sights of this part of London.

Bar food (11(12 Sun)-10) ~ Restaurant ~ (020) 7222 5577 ~ Children in eating area of bar ~ Open 11-11; 12-10.30 Sun; cl 25 Dec

33. EBURY WINE BAR
Ebury Street, SW1; ⊖/⇌ Victoria

London's first wine bar (opened 1959 – we've known it since 1962) and still one of the best, with an excellent choice of wines by the glass, this welcoming place is just a short walk from Victoria Coach Station. An enticing green-painted bow window has champagne bottles arranged in height order, and a colourful window-box. A green-painted trompe l'oeil mural runs all round the long, fairly narrow room, with witty touches – a book called *Keeping Turkeys as Pets* is by Bernard Mathews, and a cupboard is transformed into a cabinet; above a dado rail the yellow-scrubbed walls have french advertisements and pictures. Cast-iron tables with wooden tops on the red tile-effect patterned floor have green padded leather café chairs; look out for the chair made out of half a barrel. On the right, the cracked wood-effect green-painted bar counter has bottles of wine on etched mirrored shelves, green-shaded brass lamps, and solidly comfortable green leather bar stools; TV. Cosily lit by spots and wall lamps, it has a pleasantly chatty atmosphere, attracting a loyal following as well visitors, and service is friendly and polite. Enjoyable modern cooking includes bar snacks such as home-made soup (£3.80), smoked salmon (£6.50), popular steak sandwich (£6.80) and omelettes (£7), with more elaborate restaurant dishes such as pork and prawn spring rolls (£5), beef and ale sausages with puy lentils or smoked haddock, prawn and spring onion risotto (£10.50), devilled spring chicken with braised chicory (£12.50), and fried bass (£15.75).

Bar food (all day) ~ (020) 7730 5447 ~ Children allowed in daytime ~ Open 11(12 Sat)-11; 6-10 Sun; cl around 10 days Christmas and New Year

34. GRENADIER

Wilton Row, SW1; the turning off Wilton Crescent looks prohibitive, but the barrier and watchman are there to keep out cars; walk straight past – the pub is just around the corner; ⊖ Knightsbridge

One of London's most special pubs and, thanks to the active poltergeist, said to be its most haunted, this snug and very individual place is well worth the effort it can take to find it. Patriotically painted in red, white and blue, it was once the mess for the officers of the Duke of Wellington. His portrait hangs above the fireplace, alongside neat prints of Guardsmen through the ages. The bar is tiny (some might say cramped), but you should be able to plonk yourself on one of the stools or wooden benches; despite the pub's charms it rarely gets too crowded. Well kept Charles Wells Bombardier, Courage Best, Fullers London Pride and Youngs from handpumps at the rare pewter-topped bar counter; service is friendly and chatty. On Sundays, especially, you'll find several of the customers here to sample their famous bloody marys, made to a unique recipe. Bar food includes sandwiches, bowls of chips (£2) and nachos (£3.50) – very popular with after-work drinkers – good sausage and mash (£5.55), or hot steak sandwiches (£6.25); Sunday roast (£12.25). There's an intimate back restaurant. The single table in the peaceful mews outside is an ideal spot to dream of owning one of the smart little houses opposite.

Bar food (12-2, 7-9) ~ Restaurant ~ (020) 7235 3074 ~

Children in restaurant ~ Dogs allowed in bar ~ Open 12-11(10.30 Sun)

35. LORD MOON OF THE MALL

Whitehall, SW1; ⊖/⤲ Charing Cross

More individual than many Wetherspoons pubs, this well converted former bank is a useful pit-stop for families and visitors to the nearby sights. It has frequent special offers on the food, and you'd be hard-pushed to find a cheaper place to eat in the area. The impressive main room has a splendid high ceiling and quite an elegant feel, with smart old prints, big arched windows looking out over Whitehall, and a huge painting that seems to show a well-to-do 18th-c gentleman; in fact it's Tim Martin, founder of the Wetherspoons chain. Once through an arch the style is more recognisably Wetherspoons, with a couple of neatly tiled areas and bookshelves opposite the long bar; silenced fruit machines, trivia. They usually have seven or eight real ales, with the regulars generally Courage Directors, Fullers London Pride, Greene King Abbot and Shepherd Neame Spitfire; the guest beers are often very unusual, and the prices always much less than the London norm. They also keep Weston's cider. The good value bar food – served all day – is from the standard Wetherspoons menu: soup (£2.59), sandwiches (from £3.35), bangers and mash (£5.25), five bean chilli (£5.75), aberdeeen angus steak pie (£5.95), and children's meals; they usually have a 2-for-1 meal offer for £6.79. The terms of the licence rule out fried food. Efficient service. The back doors (now only an emergency exit) were apparently built as a secret entrance for the bank's account holders living in Buckingham Palace (Edward VII had an account here from the age of three); the area by here is no smoking. The pub can get busy. As you come out, Nelson's Column is immediately to the left, and Big Ben a walk of ten minutes or so to the right.

Bar food (10-10; 12-9.30 Sun) ~ (020) 7839 7701 ~ Children welcome till 5 if eating ~ Open 10-11; 12-10.30 Sun

36. NAGS HEAD

Kinnerton Street, SW1; ⊖ Knightsbridge

Minutes from Harrods, but miles away in spirit, this quaint little gem is one of the most unspoilt pubs in London, genuinely characterful and atmospheric, and with the feel of an old-fashioned local in a sleepy country village. Hidden away in an attractive and peaceful mews, it rarely gets too busy or crowded, and there's a snugly relaxed and cosy feel in the small, panelled and low-ceilinged front room, where friendly regulars sit chatting around the unusual sunken bar counter. There's a log-effect gas fire in an old cooking range (seats by here are generally snapped up pretty quickly), then a narrow passage leads down steps to an even smaller back bar with stools and a mix of comfortable seats. The well kept Adnams Best, Broadside and seasonal brews are pulled on attractive 19th-c china, pewter and brass handpumps, while other interesting old features include a 1930s what-the-butler-saw machine and a one-armed bandit that takes old pennies. The piped music is rather individual: often jazz, folk or 1920s-40s show tunes. There are a few seats and a couple of tables outside. Bar food (usefully served all day) includes sandwiches, ploughman's or plenty of salads (from £5.50), sausage, mash and beans, chilli con carne, or steak and mushroom pie (all £5.95), and various roasts (£6); there's a £1.50 surcharge added to all dishes in the evenings, and at weekends. Service is friendly and efficient. Many readers will be delighted to learn they have a fairly hard-line policy on mobile phone use.

Bar food (11.30-9.30) ~ No credit cards ~
(020) 7235 1135 ~ Children in eating area of bar ~
Dogs allowed in bar ~ Open 11-11; 12-10.30 Sun

37. RED LION
Duke of York Street, SW1; ⊖ Piccadilly Circus

Perhaps central London's most perfectly preserved Victorian pub, this busy place has mirrors so dazzling, and gleaming mahogany so warm, that it's hard to believe they weren't put in yesterday. Other notable architectural features squeezed into the very small rooms include the crystal chandeliers and cut and etched windows (readers have been particularly impressed by these), and the striking ornamental plaster ceiling. Simple lunchtime snacks such as sandwiches (£2.80)

or filled baguettes (£3.50); diners have priority on a few of
the front tables, and there's a minuscule upstairs eating area.
Well kept Adnams, Bass, Fullers London Pride, Greene King
Old Speckled Hen and Tetleys on handpump; friendly
efficient service. It can be very crowded at lunchtime (try
inching through to the back room where there's sometimes
more space); many customers spill out on to the pavement, in
front of a mass of foliage and flowers cascading down the
wall. No children inside.

No credit cards ~ (020) 7321 0782 ~ Open
11.30(12 Sat)-11; cl Sun, bank hols

38. ROCKWELL

Trafalgar Hilton, Spring Gardens, Trafalgar Square, SW1;
⊖/⇌ Charing Cross

Pleasantly airy and relaxing, this stylish street-side bar
doesn't really feel like part of a hotel: it's great for a drink
after an afternoon spent exploring the National Gallery just
across the square. A mix of blue, tan and gold leather, the
cosily arranged seating is fall-asleep comfortable, with plenty
of low-backed settees and chaises longues (almost big
enough for two), giant pouffes and armchairs. The long spotlit chrome and cream bar counter, with elegant stools and
stylishly arranged flowers, shows off an incredible range of
bourbons (they've more than 100 on the menu) along its
entire length, and they do a fine range of cocktails too; taster
trays of whiskies (from £35 to £75 for rare single casks). The

short simple bar menu is served all day, with dishes such as fish and chips (£8.50), chicken wrap (£9), cheeseburger (£9.50), and a selection of tapas (£17). Spotlit pale grey columns help break up the high-ceilinged room, which is nicely lit by the huge smoked-glass windows, and lamps on glass-topped tables; one of the off-white walls has big pictures of rock icons. They have daily papers, also piped music, and screens above the bar.

Bar food (11-11(10.30 Sun)) ~ Restaurant ~ (020) 7870 2900 ~ Children allowed till about 6 ~ Open 8am(10.30 Sun)-1am ~ Bedrooms: /£155.90B

39. STAR

Belgrave Mews West, SW1, behind the German Embassy, off Belgrave Square; ⊖ Knightsbridge

Said to be where the Great Train Robbery was planned, this nicely traditional pub is one of those timeless places that are such a pleasurable surprise to find in London. A highlight in summer is the astonishing array of hanging baskets and flowering tubs outside, much more impressive than average. Outside peak times it has a pleasantly quiet and restful local feel, and it always impresses with its particularly well kept Fullers Chiswick, ESB, London Pride and seasonal brews. The small entry room, which also has the food servery, has stools by the counter and tall windows; an arch leads to a side room with swagged curtains, well polished wooden tables and chairs, heavy upholstered settles, globe lighting, and raj fans. The back room has button-back built-in wall seats, and there's a similarly furnished room upstairs. Served all day, good value straightforward bar food might include sandwiches (from £3.25), warm roast chicken, bacon and avocado salad, sausage and mash or pasta with sun-dried tomatoes, olives, garlic and cream (£6.25), and rib-eye steak (£9.95).

Bar food (12-9) ~ (020) 7235 3019 ~ Children in eating area of bar ~ Dogs allowed in bar ~ Open 11.30-11; 12-10.30 Sun

40. WESTMINSTER ARMS
Storey's Gate, SW1; ⊖ Westminster

If during a visit to this unpretentious and friendly Westminster local you see suited gents scrambling to their feet when something a bit like a telephone bell sounds, they are MPs being chased back across the road, by the division bell, to vote. The handiest local for the Houses of Parliament and the Abbey, it usually keeps an impressive range of nine real ales, generally including Adnams Best and Broadside, Brakspears PA, Fullers London Pride, Youngs, a beer brewed for the pub, and guests like Batemans, Gales HSB and Greene King Abbot; they also do decent wines, and a dozen or so malt whiskies. Usually packed after work with government staff and researchers, the plain main bar has simple old-fashioned furnishings, with proper tables on the wooden floors, and a good deal of panelling; there's not a lot of room, so come early for a seat. The food is served in the downstairs wine bar (a good retreat from the ground-floor bustle), with some of the tables in cosy booths; typical dishes include filled rolls (from £4), ploughman's (£5.50), steak and kidney pie, fish and chips or scampi (£6.50), and roast beef (£6.95). Piped music in this area, and in the more formal upstairs restaurant, but not generally in the main bar; fruit machine. There is a couple of tables by the street outside.

Bar food (12-8) ~ Restaurant (wkdy lunchtimes (not Weds)) ~ (020) 7222 8520 ~ Children welcome at wknds, in restaurant wkdays ~ Open 11-11(6 Sat); 12-6 Sun; cl Sun evening, 25–26 Dec

41. ANTELOPE

Eaton Terr; ⊖ Sloane Square

Stylish panelled local, rather superior but friendly; bare-boards elegance in main bar, tiny snug, lots of interesting prints and old advertisements, real ales such as Adnams, Fullers London Pride, Marstons Pedigree and Tetleys, good house wines, sandwiches, baked potatoes, ploughman's and one-price hot dishes; surprisingly quiet and relaxed upstairs wkdy lunchtimes, can get crowded evenings; open all day; children in eating area

42. BUCKINGHAM ARMS

Petty France; ⊖ St James's Park

Warmly welcoming Youngs local with elegant mirrors and woodwork, unusual long side corridor fitted out with elbow ledge for drinkers (and SkyTV for motor sports), well kept ales, good value food lunchtime and evening, reasonable prices, service friendly and efficient even when busy; handy for Buckingham Palace, Westminster Abbey and St James's Park; open all day

43. EBURY DINING ROOM & BRASSERIE
Pimlico Rd; ⊖ Sloane Square
Transformation of former Ebury Arms into big modern bar and dining hall, with chocolate-coloured low-backed banquettes and bentwood chairs by rows of sturdy wooden tables under halo-like hanging lights; enormous partly curved tinted windows, high ceilings, walnut-coloured boards, and a brooding décor of dark greys and browns brightened by dancing red and orange flames on light grey walls, fresh lilies, a couple of revealing black and white photographs, wall lamps and spotlights; long wood and tinted metal bar with good wine choice, Marstons Pedigree and the usual lagers, polite welcoming staff; good brasserie food (all day wknds – most people are here to eat), seafood bar with fresh seafood on ice, little back lounge area with low padded stools and low-backed settees; unobtrusive piped music; another dining room, with chandeliers, up steep carpeted stairs; open all day

44. FEATHERS
Broadway; ⊖ St James's Park
Large comfortable pub, a Scotland Yard local, bar food downstairs, restaurant up, well kept real ales; rock DJs 2nd and 4th Sats till 1am

45. FOX & HOUNDS
Passmore St/Graham Terr; ⊖ Sloane Square
Small cosy bar with well kept ales such as Adnams, Bass, Greene King IPA and Harveys, bar food, friendly landlady and staff, wall benches, big hunting prints, old sepia photographs of pubs and customers, some toby jugs, hanging plants under attractive skylight in back room, coal-

effect gas fire and organ; can be very busy Fri night, quieter wkdy lunchtimes

46. GALLERY
Lupus St; ⊖ Pimlico
Handy for Tate Britain; modern light and airy décor, attractive prints and bric-a-brac, no smoking area, Bass, Courage Best, Greene King Abbot and Shepherd Neame Spitfire, decent food; disabled access and lavatories (conventional ones downstairs)

47. GOLDEN LION
King St; ⊖ Green Park
Rather distinguished bow-fronted building opposite Christies auction rooms, well kept ales inc Fullers London Pride, decent wines by the glass, good value food inc bargain platters for two; if downstairs bar busy, seats and tables usually available both in passageway alongside or upstairs in theatre bar

48. HORSE & GROOM
Groom Pl; ⊖ Hyde Park Corner
Smart, friendly, mews-corner pub with plush seats on stripped boards, particularly well kept Shepherd Neame, personable service

49. JUGGED HARE
Vauxhall Bridge Rd/Rochester Row; ⊖/⤋ Victoria
Fullers Ale & Pie pub in converted colonnaded bank with balustraded balcony, chandelier, prints and busts; their ales kept well, friendly efficient service, decent food, no smoking back area; fruit machine, unobtrusive piped music; open all day

50. MORPETH ARMS
Millbank; ⊖ Pimlico

Roomy and comfortable, nicely preserved Victorian pub, the local for Tate Britain; some etched and cut glass, old books and prints, photographs, earthenware jars and bottles, well kept Youngs ales inc Waggle Dance, good range of food from sandwiches up, decent choice of wines, helpful well organised service even when it's packed at lunchtime (may be lots of smokers then), quieter evenings; seats outside (a lot of traffic)

51. RED LION
Parliament St; ⊖ Westminster

Interesting pub near Houses of Parliament, with division bell – used by MPs and Foreign Office staff; parliamentary cartoons and prints, well kept Tetleys, good range of snacks and meals, small, narrow, no smoking upstairs dining room; also cellar bar

52. SHAKESPEARE
Buckingham Palace Rd; ⊖/⇌ Victoria

Bright and lively since renovations, quick food service, good choice of ales

53. SHUMI
St James's St; ⊖ Green Park

High prices bring crowd-free calm to this small and elegantly modern newish bar, just round the corner from *The Economist* and near St James's Palace; sage-green or maroon leather, cool grey walls and high ceiling, big lightly smoked windows (you can see out easily but have to peer to see in), a handsome array of backlit spirits bottles, decent wines and coffee, japanese-style 'lunch boxes' from £15 (also a cheaper bar snack and glass of wine offer, and a separate restaurant); neat, helpful, informally uniformed staff, piped nightclub jazz; open all day

54. TATTERSHALL CASTLE
off Victoria Embankment; ⊖ Embankment
Converted paddle steamer – marvellous vantage point for watching river traffic and the London Eye opposite; canopied bar serveries, with snacks, barbecues and ice-creams too in summer, for both forward and aft decks with picnic-sets; nautical décor with lots of wood and brass in wardroom bar below decks, also restaurant and late-licence wknd nightclub

55. WILTON ARMS
Kinnerton St; ⊖ Knightsbridge
Pleasant and comfortable civilised local with good choice of reasonably priced food, well kept varied ales, good friendly service even when busy; back conservatory; open all day

SW3 (Chelsea/South Kensington)

56. ADMIRAL CODRINGTON
Mossop Street, SW3; ⊖ South Kensington
One of the features that most impresses at this beautifully designed place is the retractable glass roof in the sunny back dining room, which slides open in fine weather. The food in this part is very good indeed, with a changing menu offering a fresh approach to familiar dishes. Particular favourites include their salmon fishcakes (£9.75), cod baked with

tomatoes and mushrooms in a soft herb crust (£10.75), and sirloin steak or calves liver (£13.75); good puddings. It's worth booking, particularly at weekends. The more pubby bar is an effective mix of traditional and chic, with comfortable sofas and cushioned wall seats, neatly polished floorboards and panelling, spotlights in the ceiling and lamps on elegant wooden tables, a handsome central counter, sporting prints on the yellow walls, and houseplants around the big bow windows. There's a model ship in a case just above the entrance to the dining room. A separate lunchtime bar menu might include goats cheese and red peppers on ciabatta (£6.25), steak sandwich (£6.95), fish and chips (£7.50) and cottage pie (£7.95); Sunday roasts. Well kept Charles Wells Bombardier and Flowers Original on handpump, and an excellent wine list, with a decent choice by the glass; various coffees, and a range of Havana cigars, with good knowledgeable service from smartly uniformed young staff. There may be piped pop music, and it can seem noisy when busy (the dining room is quieter). At the side is a nice little terrace with tables, benches and heaters. The transformation of the pub's interior was the work of designer Nina Campbell.

Bar food (12-2.30) ~ Restaurant ~ (020) 7581 0005 ~ Open 11.30-11; cl 25-26 Dec

57. COOPERS ARMS

Flood Street, SW3; ⊖ Sloane Square, but quite a walk

Relaxed and friendly, this spacious open-plan pub has interesting furnishings that include rush-seated chapel chairs, kitchen chairs and some dark brown plush chairs on the dark stained floorboards, a mix of nice old good-sized tables, and a pre-war sideboard and dresser; also, LNER posters and maps of Chelsea and the Thames on the walls, a stuffed bear in the corner, an enormous railway clock, a fireplace with dried flowers and a tusky boar's head above it, and tea-shop chandeliers. Well kept Youngs Bitter and Special with a guest beer such as Smiles IPA on handpump, and enjoyable bar food (reflecting modern tastes alongside familiar favourites) changes daily, and might include french onion soup (£3.95), smoked mackerel pâté (£4.95), goats cheese salad (£5.75), seared king scallops (£6.95), bangers and mash (£7.95), shepherd's pie (£8), aberdeen angus steaks (£12), and puddings (£3.50); pleasant helpful staff.
Bar food (12.30-3, 6.30-9.30) ~ (020) 7376 3120 ~ Children allowed until 6pm ~ Dogs allowed in bar ~ Open 11-11; 12-10.30 Sun

58. CROSS KEYS

Lawrence Street, SW3; ⊖ Sloane Square, but some distance away

Attractive outside with foliage and flowers, this bustling Victorian pub has an appealing and roomy, high-ceilinged

flagstoned bar around the island servery, a roaring fire, all
sorts of brassware hanging from the rafters including trum-
pets and a diver's helmet, lots of atmosphere, and a good
mix of customers; there's also a light and airy conservatory-
style back restaurant, with an ironic twist to its attractive
gardening décor. Well kept Courage Directors and
Wadworths 6X on handpump, and a good choice of wines
by the glass. Enjoyable bar food includes lunchime baguettes
(chicken or steak, £5.50), and sausage and mash or spinach
and salmon fishcakes with roasted peppers (£9.50), as well
as duck liver parfait on a warm brioche with sweet chutney or
mushroom and tarragon risotto with parmesan shavings
(£5.95), fried tiger prawns with baby spinach and garlic
butter (£7), chicken breast with a blue cheese chunky salad
(£12.95), liver and bacon (£15), tuna steak salad niçoise
(£15.50), and 9oz rib-eye steak with fondant potatoes
(£16.50). Attentive young staff; piped music.
*Bar food (12-2, 7-9) ~ Restaurant ~ (020) 7349 9111 ~
Open 12-11; 12-10.30 Sun; cl bank hols, Christmas*

59. BUILDERS ARMS
Britten St; ⊖ South Kensington
Smart bistro-style pub with good food (drinkers welcomed too); in an
attractive street

60. BUNCH OF GRAPES
Brompton Rd; ⊖ Knightsbridge
Splendid Victorian local with some robust wood carving and
effusive Victorian decoration; prompt and friendly helpful service,

comfortable seats, good if not cheap food from sandwiches up, well kept real ale, very cosmopolitan customers; handy halfway point between Harrods and the V&A

61. CROWN
Dovehouse St; ⊖ South Kensington
Small modern pub with clear windows and soft pastel colours, smartly comfortable, with particularly well kept Adnams and Fullers, shortish choice of lovingly prepared, modestly priced, unpretentious food, and friendly, speedy, unobtrusive service; won't appeal to traditionalists – two TVs with different sports events, prominent fruit machine, perhaps piped pop music

62. HENRY J BEANS
Kings Rd; ⊖ Sloane Square
Spacious bar in ornate mock-Tudor building, decent wines, Shepherd Neame Spitfire, pricy but splendid range of whiskies, other spirits, lagers and bottled beers, good value US-flavour bar food; well spaced tables, fine collection of enamelled advertising signs, keen young staff, the biggest sheltered courtyard garden of any central London pub, with its own summer bar; open all day, provision for children

63. HOUR GLASS
Brompton Rd; ⊖ Knightsbridge
Small pub handy for V&A and other nearby museums, well kept Fullers, freshly squeezed orange juice, good value food (not Sun) from speciality toasted sandwiches and baguettes to straightforward hot dishes, welcoming landlady and quick young staff; sports TV, can be a bit smoky; pavement tables

64. PHOENIX
Smith St; ⊖ Sloane Square

Newly reworked as a light and airy, comfortably modern, two-room bar mixing plush sofas and low tables by the open fire with leatherette chairs and dining tables; Battersea beer and good range of wines by the glass, up-to-date food from good lunchtime light dishes such as ciabattas to a full menu; tables outside

65. SURPRISE
Christchurch Terr; ⊖ South Kensington or Sloane Square

Friendly, eclectic and enjoyably unassuming, with well kept ales inc Fullers London Pride, decent food, and cheerful broad-spectrum mix of locals; often surprisingly quiet evenings (this is a hidden corner of Chelsea), cosy and warm; not overly done up considering location, attractive stained-glass lanterns, mural around top of bar; well behaved dogs on leads, some tables outside

W1 (West End/Soho)

66. ARGYLL ARMS
Argyll Street W1; ⊖ Oxford Circus, opposite tube side exit

A useful retreat from the hordes of Oxford Street, this bustling Victorian pub is far nicer and much more individual than its situation might lead you to expect. The most atmospheric and unusual part is the three cubicle rooms at the front, much as they were when built in the 1860s; all oddly angular, they're made by wooden partitions with very distinctive frosted and engraved glass, with hops trailing above. A long mirrored

corridor leads to the spacious back room, with the food counter in one corner. Served all day, the blackboard food includes good sandwiches and filled baguettes (from £3.95), and hot dishes such as steak and kidney pie, a daily roast, or fish and chips (£6.95). Well kept Adnams, Fullers London Pride and Greene King Old Speckled Hen on handpump; also several malt whiskies. Service is generally prompt and friendly; two fruit machines, piped music (louder in the evenings than at lunch, and very loud indeed at times). Open during busier periods, the quieter upstairs bar overlooks the pedestrianised street – and the Palladium theatre if you can see through the impressive foliage outside the window; divided into several snugs with comfortable, plush, easy chairs, it has swan's-neck lamps, and lots of small theatrical prints along the top of the walls. The gents' has a copy of the day's *Times* or *Financial Times* on the wall. The pub can get very crowded (and can seem less distinctive on busier evenings), but there's space for drinking outside.
Bar food (11-10; 12-9.30 Sun) ~ (020) 7734 6117 ~ Open 11-11; 12-10.30 Sun; cl 25 Dec

67. ATLANTIC
Glasshouse Street, W1; ⊖ Piccadilly Circus
A shortish stone's throw from Piccadilly Circus, this eye-opening basement bar is a place to be seen in these days – indeed, on busy nights having a famous or striking face may be a useful passport. By day, though, it's calm and restful –

your sense of anticipation rising as you wind down those stairs with their humming-bird wallpaper, to a big lobby under a showpiece chandelier's cascades of crystal. The main bar (there's also a little Dick's Bar) is an extensive deco ballroom with fat Carrara marble pillars, deeply comfortable, red plush banquettes and armchairs around drum tables on the near-black carpet around its edges, a lofty gold-corniced coffered ceiling, large decorative mirrors and cocktail-lounge pictures on dark green walls, period lighting and big flower arrangements. There are a few stools, and much more standing space on the shiny black floor, at the huge oval central bar, where the coolers seem to have more champagne than beer. They do good cocktails and coffee, and have lots of strong continental lagers and decent wines by the glass, including reasonably priced house wines. Bar food includes chicken satay or king prawns in filo (£6.50), burger with game chips (£8.50) and a platter of cheeses or six Falmouth rock oysters (£12); the maroon-walled part beyond the bar counter is laid out as a restaurant area, and a separate smart grill room concentrates on scotch beef from the Buccleuch estate. Service is punctilious, they have numerous copies of the *Independent*, and on our lunchtime visit, well reproduced vaguely easternish piped music was being played, quite loud (what looks like a former hat-check alcove by the door is now kitted out for evening DJs, with a vivid firework-burst-on-black décor). The lavatories are worth a look. No under-21s.

Bar food (12-2am) ~ Restaurant ~ (020) 7734 4888 ~ No children ~ Open 12-3am; cl Sun, a few days over Christmas and New Year

68. DOG & DUCK

Bateman Street, on corner with Frith Street, W1;
⊖ Tottenham Court Road or Leicester Square

A real Soho landmark, this pint-sized corner house is currently very popular with *Good Pub Guide* readers, many of whom feel it's stayed essentially unchanged for 40 years. On the floor near the door is an engaging mosaic showing a dog with its tongue out in hot pursuit of a duck; the same theme is embossed on some of the shiny tiles that frame the heavy old advertising mirrors. The main bar really is tiny, though at times manages to squeeze in a surprisingly large number of people. There are some high stools by the ledge along the back wall, and further seats in a slightly roomier area at one end. The unusual little bar counter serves very well kept Fullers London Pride, Timothy Taylors Landlord, and two changing guests such as Adnams and St Austell Tribute; also Addlestone's cider. There's a fire in winter, and newspapers to read; piped music. They now serve food all day, with bar snacks such as sausage sandwiches (£4.95) and fish and chips (£6.95). In good weather, especially, most people tend to spill on to the bustling street, though there's more space in the rather cosy upstairs bar. The pub is said to be where George Orwell celebrated when the American

Book of the Month Club chose *Animal Farm* as its monthly selection. Ronnie Scott's jazz club is nearby.
Bar food (12-9) ~ (020) 7494 0697 ~ Open 12-11; 12-10.30 Sun; cl 25 Dec

69. EAGLE BAR/DINER
Rathbone Place, W1; ⊖ Oxford Circus

A handy escape from Oxford Street's bustle, this modern bar/diner is great for post-retail therapy. The stainless steel bar with purple back-lighting (big ceiling luminaires are lit with the same colour) has rows of cocktail bottles, and deeply padded brown leather bar stools to perch on, as well as plenty of space for standing. Brown leather built-in banquettes face this bar, sharing chunky tables with red, brown and green leather cubes and chrome ladderback chairs on the marble-effect tiles; there are some more chairs by the windows, along with comfortable black leather settees and glass tables. A few steps up, and partly divided off by a solid zig-zag balustrade, dark green leather banquettes line two walls, forming cosy booths lit by solid-looking square black hanging lamps. In the evening (when it's popular with a young crowd and there may be DJs), the emphasis is on their interesting, though not cheap, drinks; as well as various cocktails, they do alcoholic milkshakes. Besides a full cooked breakfast (£6.75) and pancakes (from £4.50), the chrome menus list american-style dishes such as hot dogs (£4), sandwiches (from £6.75), and good meaty burgers with a couple of unusual varieties such as emu and black pepper, tuna or ostrich and cranberry (from £5.25), and rib-eye steak (£9), with enormous chunky chips (£2.75); they do take-aways too. The light-coloured walls have black and white urban photographs and a big Coca-Cola sign, and spotlights, with evening candles, give soft lighting. Service is relaxed; piped music; cheerful red and white tiled lavatories.

Bar food (all day) ~ (020) 7637 1418 ~ Children allowed till around 9pm ~ Open 12(10 Sat)-11; 11-6 Sun; cl 25–26 Dec

70. GRAPES

Shepherd Market, W1; ⊖ Green Park

Well-liked by regulars for its characterful atmosphere and welcoming coal fire, this chatty and engagingly old-fashioned pub is in the heart of Shepherd Market, one of central London's best-kept secrets. The dimly lit bar has a nicely traditional feel, with plenty of plush red furnishings, stuffed birds and fish in glass display cases, wooden floors and panelling, and a snug little alcove at the back. One small area is no smoking. On sunny evenings smart-suited drinkers spill out on to the square outside. A good range of six or seven well kept (though fairly pricy) beers on handpump usually takes in Boddingtons, Bass, Flowers IPA, Fullers London Pride, Marstons Pedigree and Wadworths 6X; fruit machine. No food, but, very appealingly, they say that customers are welcome to bring in their own. Service can slow down a little at the busiest times; it's much quieter at lunchtimes.

Open 11(12 Sat)-11; 12-10.30 Sun

71. GUINEA

Bruton Place, W1; ⊖ Bond Street or Green Park

Not to be confused with the quite separate upscale Guinea Grill which takes up much of the same building (uniformed doormen will politely redirect you if you've picked the entrance to that by mistake), this handily positioned little pub can still impress with its lunchtime bar food: their elaborate grilled ciabattas (from £4.95) and tasty steak and kidney pie (Mon-Fri, £10.50) have both won awards, though it's the latter that's the best known – and which for some is very much the main reason for coming. Dating back in part to the 17th c and with a history that goes back to the 15th, the pub used to cater for the servants and stable hands of the big houses in Mayfair. Like the Grenadier in SW1, it's hidden away in a smart mews, and is pretty much standing room only. Three cushioned wooden seats and tables are tucked to the left of the entrance to the bar, with a couple more in a snug area at the back, underneath a big old clock. Most people tend to prop themselves against a little shelf running along the side of the small room, or stand outside in the street, where there are another couple of tables. Well kept Youngs Bitter, Special, and seasonal brews from the striking bar counter, which has some nice wrought-iron work above it. The look of the place is appealingly simple, with bare boards, yellow walls, old-fashioned prints, and a red-planked ceiling with raj fans, but the atmosphere is chatty and civilised, with plenty of suited workers from Mayfair offices.

Bar food (12-2.30 Mon-Fri only) ~ Restaurant ~
(020) 7409 1728 ~ Children over 10 in restaurant ~ Open
11-11; 6.30-11 Sat; cl Sat lunchtime, Sun, bank hols

72. MATCH BAR
Margaret Street, W1; ⊖ Oxford Circus

Pleasantly packed in the evenings, but often almost deserted earlier in the day, this well run place is the nicest of a small London bar group best known for its excellent cocktails. The imaginative range takes in all the classics, as well as new concoctions created by their own team. The beers are unusual too; they've tried out various brews over the years, but the current ones – four uncommon and particularly distinctive bottled lagers from Greenwich's Meantime Brewing Company – are by far the best. Bar staff are friendly and helpful, and know what they're doing; there's table service, even for drinks. Long, narrow and softly lit, the bar is on two levels, with tables set for eating in a more intimate raised area, and plenty of space below – it stretches back much further than you'd think from outside. Perhaps the most comfortable bit is an almost-hidden little room at the end, with a very chilled feel and plenty of soft furnishings. Available all day, bar food includes snacks like home-made beef and chorizo burger with red onion salsa or roast salmon and haddock fishcakes (£7.50), and their Big Bowls such as sausage casserole, pumpkin and zucchini pappardelle, or braised oriental pork: designed for sharing, these come in various sizes, to suit one person (£7) or four (£20). It's quite loud in the evenings, with a cheery cacophony of music and laid-back chatter; it can be a little smoky then too. They have similar bars in Clerkenwell and Shoreditch.

Bar food (all day) ~ (020) 7499 3443 ~ DJs Thurs, Fri and Sat ~ Open 11-12; cl Sun

73. RED LION

Waverton Street, W1; ⊖ Green Park

In one of Mayfair's quietest and prettiest corners, this smartly cosy old place is well liked by *Good Pub Guide* readers for its very relaxed and distinctly un-London atmosphere. On some evenings after work it can be very busy indeed, but it always keeps its comfortably civilised feel, and has something of the air of a popular country local. The main L-shaped bar has small winged settles on the partly carpeted scrubbed floorboards, and London prints below the high shelf of china on its dark-panelled walls. Well kept beers such as Charles Wells Bombardier, Courage Directors, Fullers London Pride and Greene King IPA on handpump, and they do rather good bloody marys (with a daunting Very Spicy option); also a dozen or so malt whiskies. Bar food, served from a corner at the front, includes sandwiches (from £3), ploughman's (£4.50), sausage and mash (£4.95), cod and chips, half-rack of grilled pork ribs or cajun chicken (all £6.95), and specials such as mushroom stroganoff. Unusually for this area, they serve food morning and evening seven days a week. The gents' usually has a copy of *Private Eye* at eye level (it used to be the *Financial Times*). On Saturday evenings they generally have a pianist.

Bar food (12-3, 6-9.30) ~ Restaurant ~ (020) 7499 1307 ~ Children in eating area of bar and restaurant ~ Dogs allowed in bar ~ Piano Sat evening ~ Open 11.30-11; 6-11 Sat; 12-3, 6-10.30 Sun; cl Sat am

74. TOUCAN
Carlisle Street, W1; ⊖ Tottenham Court Road

Just around the corner from Soho Square, it's the basement bar here, easy-going and not smart, which is special. You can get straight to it off the pavement, by the iron steps down into the area. It's very small, so can get crowded for the main lunchtime and early evening sessions; other times find it at its most relaxed, with space to enjoy the vintage Guinness advertisements, and the murals of toucans, life-size and larger, which cover the walls. Five taps are devoted to that classic drink, and with it you can have six Rossmore oysters (£6); or the friendly and professional barman will guide you knowledgeably through his exceptional range of irish whiskeys. Other well priced food includes sandwiches (from £2.50), baked potatoes (from £3.50), steak and kidney pie (made with Guinness, of course) or sausage and champ

(£5.95), and perhaps irish stew; and the piped music is of the sort that's popular in Ireland, not necessarily the same thing as 'irish music'. The furniture on the plain tiled floor seems designed to keep you sober: you need to preserve at least some sense of balance to perch securely on the huge round cushions of those bongo drum-shaped bar stools, let alone the fat pads precariously topping some disused kegs. They also have a handful of tables with small bentwood stools. There is an unobtrusive TV, with another in the plain upstairs bar – which overflows on to the pavement when it's busy. *Bar food (11-5) ~ (020) 7437 4123 ~ Open 11-11 Mon-Sat; cl Sun, 25-26 Dec*

75. WAXY O'CONNORS
Rupert Street, W1; ⊖ Piccadilly Circus

The small street entry takes you into a surprising maze of dark cavernous rooms, up and down several flights of steps, wriggling right through to Wardour St (and another entrance). In the three serving bars, rows of Guinness taps are prominent (they have a few wines by the glass, and do teas and coffees), as are the irish football jerseys behind the bar, and the irish piped music. The décor is rich in gothic reclaimed woodwork, carving and curly wrought iron, with stripped stone and bare boards, flickering wall lights, candles, candelabra and flame-effect stoves – in some places it looks like a Disneyesque monastery, in others, with balconies, earth-coloured burrowings and bare branches,

Hobbits come to mind. The young staff are friendly, and enjoyable food might include soup (£3.50), filled potato skins or ciabattas (from £5.50), sausage and mash, burger or six Rossmore oysters (£6.95) and rib-eye steak (£7.95); one area is set as a restaurant. Though there's plenty of room by day, it can get packed with young people at night, and very loud then, as the acoustics are very lively; they also have frequent live bands. If you're up at the top, it's a long, long way down to the lavatories.

Bar food (12-7) ~ Open 12(11 Sat)-11; 12-10.30 Sun; cl 25 Dec

76. AUDLEY
Mount St; ⊖ Green Park
Classic civilised Mayfair pub; opulent red plush, High Victorian mahogany and engraved glass, clock hanging in lovely carved wood bracket from ornately corniced ceiling; well kept Courage Best and Directors from long polished bar, good food and service, good coffee, upstairs panelled dining room; open all day

77. BARLEY MOW
Dorset St; ⊖ Baker Street
Built in 1791, a pub when Marylebone was still a village; attractive, unspoilt and cosy, with Greene King IPA, Marstons Pedigree and Tetleys, spotless housekeeping, panelling, old pictures; three unusual 19th-c cubicles opening on to serving counter, in which the poor old farmers could pawn their watches to the landlord in private; pavement café tables

78. BOHÈME KITCHEN & BAR
Old Compton St; ⊖ Leicester Square

In Soho's heart – you really feel it if you manage to nab a table by the big streetside windows; lively and bustling even at fairly quiet times, low ceilings and lighting, light grey walls, plenty of dark wood, comfortable brown leather seats lining one wall, some low leather cubes, unusual cone-shaped wooden bar stools, with drinking space around island serving bar; good strong coffee, the usual foreign-name lagers and so forth, efficient service; most tables set for the well presented food (at Soho prices), from sandwiches and burgers to seafood inc lobster; trendy piped music

79. CLACHAN
Kingly St; ⊖ Oxford Circus

Neat, recently refurbished pub behind Liberty's, lovely wooden bar, ornate plaster ceiling supported by two large fluted and decorated pillars, comfortable screened leather banquettes, smaller drinking alcove up three or four steps; Adnams, Fullers London Pride and Greene King IPA, good service from hard-working smart staff, above-average food inc once-common now-rare pub snacks such as scotch eggs and pork pies; can get busy, but very relaxed in afternoons

80. COCK
Great Portland St; ⊖ Oxford Circus

Large corner local with enormous lamps over picnic-sets outside, florid Victorian/Edwardian décor with tiled floor, handsome woodwork, some cut and etched glass, high tiled ceiling, ornate plasterwork, velvet curtains, coal-effect gas fire; well kept cheap Sam Smiths OB from all four handpumps, popular lunchtime food in upstairs lounge with two more coal-effect gas fires

81. COUCH
Dean St; ⊖ Tottenham Court Road
Big-windowed, high-ceilinged bar, relaxed and popular in the evenings, with lots of space for drinking or eating; chapel chairs around sturdy wooden tables on dark boards, with built-in settees in two corners; a little lounge area on the right has a comfortably well worn leather settee and armchairs, with daily papers on a big coffee table; butter-coloured walls, big mirrors, a scattering of photos and cartoons, a couple of big pot plants, old-fashioned golden chandeliers, and chrome wall lamps; lagers on tap and cocktails from the long bar counter to the right; blackboards listing an enjoyable range of food; TV, funky piped music

82. CROBAR
Manette St; ⊖ Tottenham Court Road
Trendy bar with good rock jukebox – and very handy for the good nostalgic rock acts at the Borderline

83. DE HEMS
Macclesfield St; ⊖ Leicester Square
Typical London pub recycled as unusual pastiche of a dutch bar, old dutch engravings, big continental founts and good range of interesting bottled beers, friendly bar service, plenty of room

84. DOVER CASTLE
Weymouth Mews; ⊖ Regents Park
Simple yet quite elegant and comfortable, with some panelling and old prints, charming back snug, cheap Sam Smiths OB; can be quiet, but piped music may obtrude

85. FITZROVIA
Goodge St/Whitfield St; ⊖ Goodge Street

Attractively priced food from soup and sandwiches up, Fullers London Pride, Greene King IPA and Charles Wells Bombardier; nice atmosphere and interesting mix of customers; picnic-sets outside

86. FITZROY
Charlotte St; ⊖ Goodge Street

Tidy pub with photographs of customers Augustus John, Dylan Thomas and the young Richard Attenborough, George Orwell's NUJ card and so forth; carpeted downstairs bar with white-painted brickwork, wooden settles and a couple of snugs, comfortable upstairs bar; low-priced Sam Smiths OB, good value food inc filled baguettes, expert friendly staff; may be piped music; plenty of tables out under cocktail parasols, popular in summer

87. GOLDEN EAGLE
Marylebone Lane; ⊖ Bond Street

Tastefully renovated Victorian pub with traditional features but modern feel; well kept beers such as Brakspears, Fullers London Pride and St Austell, fresh flowers, friendly service; piano singalong Thurs

88. LAMB & FLAG
James St/Barratt St; ⊖ Bond Street

Pleasant bare-boards pub with panelling and low, ribbed and bossed ceiling, friendly staff; Courage Directors, Fullers London Pride, Greene King IPA, Marstons Pedigree and Charles Wells Bombardier from attractive bar counter with barley-sugar pillars supporting coloured leaded glass; decent wines, plain hot dishes

89. MARKET PLACE
Market Pl; ⊖ Oxford Circus
Sharing its off-Oxford St pedestrian enclave with several other bars, cafés and restaurants, this big-windowed newish bar has robust tables and benches of unsealed wood and roughly welded steel, plus lots of bare wood planking with signs branded in by hot pokers; trendy food strong on interesting sharing platters and using free-range meats from a brightly stainless-steel open kitchen, and plenty of cocktails, wines and coffees as well as the usual lagers and so forth; a second basement bar has a DJ station (by day there may be rather muffled piped music), and leather banquettes in yellow barrel-vaulted cellar alcoves; pavement tables, open till 1am Fri and Sat

90. NEWMAN ARMS
Rathbone St/Newman Passage; ⊖ Goodge Street
Fullers and Youngs (unusual combination) kept well in small panelled bar with nautical memorabilia and good service; home-made pies in small room upstairs

91. O'CONOR DON
Marylebone Lane; ⊖ Bond Street
Enjoyable and civilised, family-run bare-boards pub, genuinely and unobtrusively irish, with pubby tables and chairs on dark bare boards, elbow shelf right around frosted glass windows, and high plastered ceiling; good baguettes and other freshly made bar food, waitress drinks service (to make sure the Guinness has settled properly), warm bustling atmosphere, daily papers; may be piped 1970s pop music; good upstairs restaurant with daily fresh Galway oysters; folk music Sat; handy for the Wallace Collection

92. OLD COFFEE HOUSE
Beak St; ⊖ Piccadilly Circus

Polished pub with masses of interesting bric-a-brac, unusually wide choice of decent lunchtime food (not Sun) in upstairs room full of prints and pictures, well kept real ales; fruit machine, piped music; children allowed upstairs 12-3, open all day exc Sun afternoon; very popular with wknd shoppers and tourists

93. RED LION
Kingly St; ⊖ Oxford Circus

Friendly, solidly modernised without being spoilt, narrow front bar, darts behind, well kept low-priced Sam Smiths; short realistically priced lunchtime food choice in comfortable room upstairs; video jukebox

94. REVOLUTION
St Annes Ct; ⊖ Tottenham Court Road

Part of a countrywide chain of vodka bars, with a huge range of vodkas (they even have Bakewell tart flavour), various drinks offers (inc six shots for £10), cocktails, and continental lagers on tap; relaxed by day, but packed Fri and Sat evenings (when there are bouncers, and you may struggle to get in, let alone find a seat); dimly lit with black lamps, spotlights and candles on some tables, lots of dark wood with panelled windows, long studded metal bar counter, and industrial-style black ceiling; a good-sized standing area (partly divided off by a low balcony) and a thoughtful range of places to sit from intimate tables for two, to comfortable black and brown leather settees (just right for a lively group) on a red carpet under blue and pink spotlights, also leather cubes, built-in wall banquettes and sturdy bar stools; straightforward food inc an all-day breakfast and sharing platters, daily papers; piped music (loud at night), regular DJs

95. RUNNING FOOTMAN
Charles St; ⊖ Green Park
Bow window, dark panelling, ochre ceiling, painting of the epony-
mous footman over fireplace, real ales inc Shepherd Neame Spitfire;
a comfortable crush of happy customers

96. YORKSHIRE GREY
Langham St; ⊖ Oxford Circus
Small bare-boards corner pub with well kept cheap Sam Smiths OB,
lots of wood, bric-a-brac and prints, comfortable seating inc snug
little parlour; friendly staff, attractively priced bar lunches; open all
day

W2 (Bayswater/Paddington)

97. ARCHERY TAVERN
Bathurst Street, W2, opposite the Royal Lancaster Hotel;
⊖ Lancaster Gate
Changing manager just as we went to press, this welcoming
and nicely kept Victorian pub is a useful stop for visitors to
this side of Hyde Park. Taking its name from an archery
range that occupied the site for a while in the early 19th c, it
has plenty of space, and all sorts of types and ages can be
found chatting quietly in the several comfortably relaxing,
pubby areas around the central servery. On the green
patterned walls are a number of archery prints, as well as a
history of the pub and the area, other old prints, dried hops,

and quite a few plates lined along a shelf. Well kept Badger Best, King & Barnes and Tanglefoot on handpump. A big back room has long tables, bare boards and a fireplace; darts, TV, a big stack of board games, fruit machine, piped music. Bar food has included things like sandwiches, soup, daily specials such as chicken, leek and stilton pie (£5.75), and 8oz rump steak (£6.95); they may do breakfasts on weekend mornings. There's lots more seating in front of the pub, under hanging baskets and elaborate floral displays, and some nicely old-fashioned lamps. A side door leads on to a little mews, where the Hyde Park Riding Stables are based.

Bar food (12-2.30(3 Sun), 6-9) ~ (020) 7402 4916 ~ Children welcome ~ Dogs welcome ~ Open 11-11; 12-10.30 Sun

98. MAD BISHOP & BEAR
Paddington Station; ⊖/≋ Paddington

Up escalators from concourse in new part of station, classic city pub décor in cream and pastels, ornate plasterwork, etched mirrors and fancy lamps inc big brass chandeliers, parquet, tiles and carpet, booths with leather banquettes, lots of wood and prints; a guest beer and full Fullers beer range kept well from long counter, good wine choice, friendly smartly dressed staff, wide choice of good value food from breakfast (7.30 on) and sandwiches to Sun roasts; big no smoking area, train departures screen, soft piped music, fruit machine; open all day, tables out overlooking concourse

99. VICTORIA
Strathearn Pl; ⊖ Lancaster Gate

Interesting and well preserved corner local, lots of Victorian Royal and other memorabilia, *Vanity Fair* cartoons and unusual little military paintings, two cast-iron fireplaces, wonderful gilded mirrors and mahogany panelling, brass mock-gas lamps above attractive horseshoe bar, bare boards and banquettes; relaxed atmosphere, friendly attentive service, full Fullers range kept well, good choice of wines by the glass, well priced food counter; upstairs has leather club chairs in small library/snug (and, mostly used for private functions now, replica of Gaiety Theatre bar, all gilt and red plush); quiet piped music, TV (off unless you ask); pavement picnic-sets

WC1 (Holborn/Bloomsbury)

100. CITTIE OF YORKE
High Holborn, WC1; find it by looking out for its big black and gold clock; ⊖ Chancery Lane

Like a vast baronial hall, the main back bar of this unique pub takes your breath away when seen for the first time. Vast thousand-gallon wine vats rest above the gantry, big bulbous lights hang from the soaring high-raftered roof, and an extraordinarily extended bar counter stretches off into the distance. It can get packed, particularly in the early evening, particularly with lawyers and City folk, but it's at busy times like these when the pub seems most magnificent. Most people tend to congregate in the middle, so you may still be able to bag one of the intimate, old-fashioned and ornately carved booths that run along both sides. The triangular Waterloo fireplace, with grates on all three sides and a figure of Peace among laurels, used to stand in the Hall of Grays Inn Common Room until less obtrusive heating was introduced (thanks to those who sent us more thorough notes on its history). Well kept Sam Smiths OB on handpump (appealingly priced at around a pound less than the typical cost of a London pint); friendly service from smartly dressed staff, fruit machine and piped music in the cellar bar. A smaller, comfortable panelled room has lots of little prints of York and attractive brass lights, while the ceiling of the entrance hall has medieval-style painted panels and plaster York roses. Served all day from buffet counters in the main hall and cellar bar, bar food includes sandwiches (from £3.25), and half a dozen daily-changing hot dishes such as steak and kidney pie or lasagne (£4.95). A pub has stood on this site since 1430, though the current building owes more to the 1695 coffee house erected here behind a garden; it was reconstructed in Victorian times, using 17th-c materials and parts.

Bar food (12-9) ~ (020) 7242 7670 ~ Children in eating area of bar ~ Open 11.30(12 Sat)-11; cl Sun, bank hols

101. LAMB

Lamb's Conduit Street, WC1; ⊖ Holborn

One of the capital's most famous pubs, this old favourite has been particularly praised by *Good Pub Guide* readers over

the last year. Best known for its unique Victorian fittings and atmosphere, it's especially nice after lunch when the crowds have gone and you can better appreciate its timeless charms. The highlight is the bank of cut-glass swivelling 'snob-screens' all the way around the U-shaped bar counter, but sepia photographs of 1890s actresses on the ochre panelled walls, and traditional cast-iron-framed tables with neat brass rails around the rim, all add to the overall effect. Consistently well kept Youngs Bitter, Special and seasonal brews on handpump, along with a guest such as Smiles Best, and around 40 different malt whiskies; thoughtful service. Lunchtime bar food includes a popular hot ham baguette (£4.75), with the meat carved on the counter, as well as ploughman's (£4.75), vegetable curry (£5.75), sausage and mash (£5.95), fish and chips (£6.35), beef and ale pie (£6.95), and lemon and tarragon chicken (£8.50); popular Sunday roasts (£6.75). Shove-ha'penny, cribbage, dominoes; no machines or music. A snug room at the back on the right is no smoking, and there are slatted wooden seats in a little courtyard beyond. It can get very busy, especially in the evenings. Like the street, the pub is named for the Kentish clothmaker William Lamb who brought fresh water to Holborn in 1577. Note: they don't allow children. *Bar food (12-2.30, 6-9(not Sun evening)) ~*
(020) 7405 0713 ~ Open 11-11; 12-4, 7-10.30 Sun

102. MUSEUM TAVERN

Museum Street/Great Russell Street, WC1; ⊖ Holborn or Tottenham Court Road

Supposed to have been a favourite with Karl Marx, this unspoilt and quietly civilised Victorian pub is directly opposite the British Museum. The single room is simply furnished and decorated, with high-backed wooden benches around traditional cast-iron pub tables, and old advertising mirrors between the wooden pillars behind the bar. Lunchtime tables are sometimes hard to come by, and there can be an initial crush after work, but at other times it can be pleasantly uncrowded in the evenings, with a nicely peaceful atmosphere in late afternoons. A decent choice of well kept beers usually takes in Charles Wells Bombardier, Courage Directors, Fullers London Pride, Theakstons Old Peculier, and Youngs Original and Special; they also have several wines by the glass, a choice of malt whiskies, and tea, coffee, cappuccino and hot chocolate. Good service. From a servery at the end of the room, straightforward bar food might include sandwiches (from £3.45), pie or quiche with salads, fish and chips (£6.75), and Sunday roasts. There are one or two tables out under the gas lamps and 'Egyptian' inn sign. *Bar food (11-3.30, 5-9.30) ~ (020) 7242 8987 ~ Open 11-11; 12-10.30 Sun*

103. CALTHORPE ARMS
Grays Inn Rd; ⊖ Chancery Lane
Consistently well kept Youngs Bitter, Special and seasonal beer at sensible prices in relaxed and unpretentious corner pub with plush wall seats; big helpings of popular food upstairs lunchtime and evening; nice pavement tables; open all day

104. DOLPHIN
Red Lion St; ⊖ Holborn
Small, cosy and welcoming, high stools and wide shelves around the walls, old photographs, horsebrasses, hanging copper pots and pans and so forth inside; simple lunchtime food, and real ales such as Bass, Boddingtons, Brakspears and Fullers London Pride; seats and flower-filled windowboxes outside; open all day wkdys, plus Sat lunchtime

105. DUKE OF YORK
Roger St; ⊖ Chancery Lane
Quietly placed and unpretentious, with Formica-top tables and café chairs on patterned lino downstairs, real ales such as Greene King Old Speckled Hen and Ind Coope Burton, helpful staff, cool and welcoming young atmosphere (big Andy Warhol-style pictures); can be smoky; emphasis on surprisingly good and interesting modern food at reasonable prices, upstairs dining room

106. NA ZDROWIE
Little Turnstile; ⊖ Holborn
Homely little polish bar, tucked down an alley; sparsely decorated, with sunshine yellow and light blue walls with polish eagle emblems, and a large transfer of an eagle on one grey wall, dark cream ceiling, and partly opaque windows; the grey-painted floor has yellow plastic-topped bar stools to perch on, tall round bar tables, silver chairs and dark blue pouffes around a couple of café tables;

dark wooden-topped metal bar counter with a great choice of vodkas, a couple of lagers, and interesting polish dishes from a little serving hatch behind the bar; open 12.30(6 Sat)-11; cl Sun

107. PAKENHAM ARMS
Pakenham St; ⊖/⇌ Kings Cross
Relaxed unspoilt split-level local, quiet at lunchtime and wknds; well kept real ales, friendly staff, generous food, big open doors making it light and airy in summer; picnic-sets outside, lots of flowers

108. PLOUGH
Museum St/Little Russell St; ⊖ Tottenham Court Road
Neatly kept two-bar Bloomsbury local with well kept beer, daily papers; upstairs no smoking room with food such as baked potatoes, ploughman's, salads, sausage and mash, and pasta

109. PRINCESS LOUISE
High Holborn; ⊖ Holborn
Etched and gilt mirrors, brightly coloured and fruity-shaped tiles, slender Portland stone columns, lofty and elaborately colourful ceiling, quiet plush-seated corners; attractively priced Sam Smiths from the long counter, good friendly service, simple bar snacks, upstairs lunchtime buffet; notable Victorian gents'; crowded and lively during the week, with great evening atmosphere – usually quieter late evening, or Sat lunchtime; open all day, cl Sun

110. RUGBY
Great James St; ⊖ Holborn
Sizeable corner pub with well kept Shepherd Neame ales inc their seasonal beer, usual food, good service; tables outside

111. SWINTONS
Swinton St; ⊖/⚊ Kings Cross
Former Kings Head converted to enjoyable dining pub; relaxing ambience, extensive wine list as well as draught and bottled beer; no TVs or machines

WC2 (Covent Garden/Leicester Square)

112. CAFÉ DES AMIS
Hanover Place, just off Long Acre, WC2; ⊖ Covent Garden
This compact basement bar, right by the Royal Ballet School, has dramatic silver-framed dance and theatre photographs on most of its pale ochre walls, and many of the regular customers have ballet and theatre connections. Lighting is soft, and around the sides are dark velour banquettes and stools around solid modern tables; big smoked mirrors give an illusion of space, and down here you feel curiously and pleasantly out of time and out of place. The island bar servery has stools all around its high counter; the choice of wines by the glass (large or super-sized) is good and interesting if not cheap, and service is appealingly personal. Worthwhile food might include plates of cheese (three for £6.50, five for £8.50), toasted mozzarella and tomato ciabatta (£6.50), a particularly tasty warm chicken baguette (£7.50), tender steak sandwich or a plate of charcuterie with interestingly flavoured pâté (£8), and enterprising dishes of the day such

as prosciutto with roasted figs (£5) or duck leg confit with pumpkin rissolée (£9.50). Upstairs on the ground floor is a good more formal restaurant – for the bar, just head straight down the stairs on the left as you go in.

Bar food (all day) ~ (020) 7379 3444 ~ Children allowed till 5pm ~ Open 11.30-11; cl Sun, 25 Dec-4 Jan

113. CORK & BOTTLE

Cranbourn Street, WC2; ⊖ Leicester Square

This basement wine bar just off Leicester Square has changed little over the 30 years that we have known it. With its small and unobtrusive entrance it's easily missed, so is chiefly a haunt of the 'occasional regulars' who value it so highly for its consistently good value food and wines, cheerful service, and pleasant informal atmosphere, relaxed even at busy times. It has two main rooms, neither of them large, and a snug little side cellar area with just one table under its very low vaulted ceiling. The main areas have bentwood chairs around close-set white-clothed tables, and lots of wine advertisements on the mustard-coloured walls above a blue-painted panelled dado. Good food all day includes interesting salads and so on from a glazed display servery; there is a choice of pâtés (£5.95), or plates of three cheeses (you can chose from about 15, £7.50); they also do some hot dishes such as ham and cheese pie (£7.95), shepherd's pie with black pudding (£8.95), home-made burger (£9.95), 8oz sirloin steak (£11.95) and blackened salmon (£11.95).

The excellent wine choice includes some enterprising New World offerings. A cork board in the gents' shows today's sports pages.

Bar food (all day) ~ (020) 7734 7807 ~ Children allowed at manager's discretion ~ Open 11-11.30; cl 24-26 Dec

114. GORDONS
Villiers Street, WC2; ⊖ Embankment

This unusual place, holding its licence not in the common way but under the special privileges of the Worshipful Company of Free Vintners, has scarcely changed at all in the more than 40 years that we have known it. Go down steps to these linked stone-floored cellars, with ancient lithographs, photographs and news clippings on some walls, a venerable clocking-in machine (it still keeps time), chipped and crazed brown or ochre paint on wall and ceiling boards, blackened bricks and swollen lime mortar in arched barrel-vaulting; dim lighting including candles in bottles, and an easy-going mix of elderly tables and upright chairs. The licence doesn't cover spirits, but to compensate they do a fine range of fortified wines – ports, madeiras and sherries – by the glass, along with reasonably priced table wines. The food is simple, and these days is rather good. A cold counter shows a wide choice of cheeses (two-cheese ploughman's is £6.95), with bread and pâté (£4.50) and quite a few salads (£5.25-£7.40); they also do three or four hot dishes, such as pepper quiche (£6.95), fishcake (£7.95), cottage pie (£8.50) and

spicy chicken with bacon (£8.75). Service is obliging.
*Bar food (12-10) ~ (020) 7930 1408 ~ Children welcome ~
Open 11-11; 12-10 Sun*

115. LAMB & FLAG

Rose Street, WC2, off Garrick Street; ⊖ Leicester Square

A Californian correspondent considers his trips to London complete only after a visit to this ever-popular old place, a pub of great charm and character with an eventful and well documented history: Dryden was nearly beaten to death by hired thugs outside, and Dickens made fun of the Middle Temple lawyers who frequented it when he was working in nearby Catherine St. Unspoilt and in places rather basic, it's enormously popular with after-work drinkers and visitors; it can be empty at 5pm and heaving by 6, and even in winter you'll find an overflow of people drinking and chatting in the little alleyways outside. Access throughout has been improved in recent years; the more spartan front bar now leads easily into the back, without altering too much the snug feel of the place. The low-ceilinged back bar has high-backed black settles and an open fire, and in Regency times was known as the Bucket of Blood from the bare-knuckle prize-fights held here. Well kept Courage Best and Directors, Charles Wells Bombardier, Youngs Special and changing guests on handpump; as in most pubs round here, the beer isn't cheap, but on weekdays between 11 and 5 you should find at least one offered at a substantial saving. Also, a good

few malt whiskies. The bar food – lunchtimes only – is simple but good value, with good sandwiches, filled baked potatoes (£3.50), and half a dozen main courses such as macaroni cheese (£3.95), spicy cumberland sausages or lamb hot pot (£4.25), and a choice of roasts (£5.95). The upstairs Dryden Room is often quieter than downstairs, and has jazz every Sunday evening; there's a TV in the front bar.
Bar food (11(12 Sun)-3) ~ No credit cards ~
(020) 7497 9504 ~ Children in eating area of bar ~ Jazz
Sun evenings ~ Open 11-11(10.45 Fri and Sat); 12-10.30
Sun; cl 25 Dec, 1 Jan

116. MOON UNDER WATER
Charing Cross Road, WC2; ⊖ Tottenham Court Road or Leicester Square
Now opening at 10am for breakfast, this enormous place is another Wetherspoons pub, but rather different from their usual style. It's a conversion of the former Marquee Club, but rather than introducing pseudo-traditional fittings it's been done out in a dramatic, modern style, with remarkable results: big and brash, it's a perfect central London meeting point, attracting an intriguing mix of customers, from Soho trendies and students to tourists and the local after-work crowd. The carefully designed main area is what used to be the auditorium, now transformed into a cavernous white-painted room stretching far off into the distance, with seats and tables lining the walls along the way. It effortlessly absorbs the

hordes that pour in on Friday and Saturday evenings, and even when it's at its busiest you shouldn't have any trouble traversing the room, or have to wait very long to be served at the bar; indeed some regulars feel the pub is at its best when it's at its most crowded. There are normally up to ten very nicely priced real ales on handpump: Courage Directors, Fullers London Pride, Greene King Abbot, Shepherd Neame Spitfire, Theakstons Best, and several rapidly changing more unusual guests. They have regular real ale festivals and promotions, also quite a range of coffees, most of which you can buy to take away. Served all day, the good value food is the same as at other Wetherspoons pubs, with the same bargain offers: two meals for £6.49, or special prices on their weekly curry and steak nights. The former stage is the area with most seats, and from here a narrower room leads past another bar to a back door opening on to Greek Street (quite a surprise, as the complete lack of windows means you don't realise how far you've walked). A couple of areas are no-smoking, including the small seating area upstairs, with its bird's-eye view of all the comings and goings. If this kind of pub really isn't your thing, at the very least it's a handy shortcut to Soho. *Bar food (10-10.30) ~ (020) 7287 6039 ~ Open 10-11; 12-10.30 Sun*

117. SEVEN STARS

Carey Street, WC2; ⊖ Holborn (just as handy from Temple or Chancery Lane, but the walk through Lincoln's Inn Fields can be rather pleasant)

Long a favourite with lawyers and reporters covering notable trials nearby, this cosy little pub has considerably widened its appeal under the current licensees, who've introduced a greater emphasis on imaginative, home-cooked food. Served all day, the blackboard menu might include things like half a dozen oysters (£6), Country Scramble (a chunk of sourdough with smoked pork, sliced potato, onion, parsley and thyme, £7.50), chargrilled fresh whole sea bream with lemon wedges and lentil purée (£8), two grilled quails and three merguez sausages with watercress on a sourdough croûton toasted in olive oil (£8), and plenty of seasonal game; at times you may also find vintage port with fruit cake. The two unspoilt rooms have several tables set for eating, as well as plenty of caricatures of barristers and judges on the red-painted walls, posters of legal-themed British films, big ceiling fans, and a relaxed, intimate atmosphere. It can fill up very quickly, and on busy evenings customers sometimes spill on to the quiet road facing the back of the Law Courts. Well kept Adnams Best and Broadside, Fullers Organic Honeydew and Harveys Sussex Best on handpump. Service is prompt and very friendly. The Elizabethan stairs up to the lavatories are rather steep, but the licensees tell us that with the addition of a good strong handrail and some light grey rubber, the

trip is now 'a safe and bouncy delight'.
*Bar food (12-9) ~ Restaurant ~ (020) 7242 8521 ~ Dogs
allowed in bar ~ Open 11-11; 12-11.30 Sat; cl Sun, Easter
Mon, 25-26 Dec, 1 Jan, possibly other bank hols*

118. ALL BAR ONE
Leicester Sq; ⊖ Leicester Square

This is one of a chain with a good many others dotted around
London, sometimes (unlike this) converted banks and usually in areas
that are fairly busy in the evenings – when they are popular meeting
places, and the piped music may be louder; chapel chairs around
big sturdy tables on narrow stripped boards, minimalist décor of dull
green and creamy yellow, bar stools along big windows as well as
the bar counter, mezzanine seating too; reasonably priced
blackboard food from sandwiches through modern snacks to
chargrills, Adnams, Fullers London Pride, lots of continental beers
and wines (ladder access to a wall of bottles is a feature of others in
the chain); no under-21s, tables and chairs out in the pedestrianised
square

119. BIERODROME
Kingsway; ⊖ Holborn

One of a small chain specialising in belgian beers, bottled and
draught, also lots of genevers, and good choice of wines by the
glass; their good value taster trays (of beers or even schnapps)
quickly put evening groups in a cheerful party mood, and the food
has an appealing belgian slant – moules with frites and so forth;
friendly staff, daily papers; open all day

120. BROWNS
St Martins Lane; ⊖ Leicester Square
Spacious bar and restaurant in what was once the City of Westminster's County Courts; good relaxed atmosphere in bar on left with plenty of wines and lagers from very long bar counter, high ceilings and panelling, big mirrors and potted plants, alcoves of soft-cushioned green settees around low tables, steps to other areas with green wicker and bentwood seats around more tables; helpful service from neat staff, open-plan restaurant area on right, enjoyable good value food; other branches in Bath, Brighton, Cambridge, Edinburgh and Oxford

121. CHANDOS
St Martins Lane; ⊖ Leicester Square
Busy downstairs bare-boards bar with snug booths, more comfortable upstairs lounge with opera photographs, low wooden tables, panelling, leather sofas, orange, red and yellow leaded windows; well kept cheap Sam Smiths OB, prompt cheerful mainly antipodean service, basic food from sandwiches to Sun roasts; air conditioning, darts and pinball; can get packed early evening, piped music and games machines; note the automaton on the roof (working 10-2 and 4-9); children upstairs till 6pm, open all day from 9am (for breakfast)

122. CHESHIRE CHEESE
Little Essex St/Milford Lane; ⊖ Temple
Small cosy panelled pub, leaded bow windows and pretty flower boxes; friendly staff, thriving local atmosphere, cheap food, Courage and more esoteric beers; lots of police badges and shields, basement restaurant

123. COACH & HORSES
Wellington St; ⊖ Covent Garden
Small friendly and spotless irish pub with imported Dublin Guinness from old-fashioned copper-topped bar, well kept Courage Best, John Smiths and Marstons Pedigree, lots of whiskeys; barman with computer-like drinks order memory; good lunchtime hot roast beef baps; can get crowded, handy for Royal Opera House

124. COAL HOLE
Strand; ⊖/≊ Charing Cross
Pleasant and comfortable, downstairs bar with carefully revamped high ceiling (may be piped music), airy and quieter upper bar; good range of beers, decent house wine, well priced sandwiches, baked potatoes, good sausages and mash, etc; handy for Raymond Gubbay's opera

125. CROSS KEYS
Endell St/Betterton St; ⊖ Covent Garden
Friendly and cosy, refreshingly un-Londonish, with masses of of photographs and posters inc Beatles memorabilia, brasses and tasteful bric-a-brac on the dark dim-lit walls, relaxed chatty feel; impressive range of lunchtime sandwiches at sensible prices and a few hot dishes then, well kept Courage Best, Marstons Pedigree and a guest beer, quick service even at busy times; small upstairs bar, often used for functions; fruit machine, gents' downstairs; picnic-sets out on cobbles tucked behind a little group of trees, pretty flower tubs and hanging baskets; open all day

126. KNIGHTS TEMPLAR
Chancery Lane; ⊖ Chancery Lane
Elaborately decorated Wetherspoons in former bank; marble pillars, handsome fittings and plasterwork, good bustling atmosphere on two levels; up to nine well kept real ales from mainstream to rare, good wine choice, good all-day menu inc bargains, friendly staff; no smoking areas; remarkably handsome lavatories; open all day inc Sun

127. LOWLANDER
Drury Lane; ⊖ Covent Garden
Smart, well run Brussels-style bar with neat long rows of tables (one just for drinking), major beers on tap with some guests and interesting bottled beers

128. MARQUIS OF GRANBY
Chandos Pl; ⊖/⇌ Charing Cross
Small, narrow and high-ceilinged, with high stools by windows overlooking the street, cosy parlour-like areas each end through arched wood-and-glass partitions; well kept Adnams and Marstons Pedigree, reasonably priced pub food; open all day

129. NAGS HEAD
James St/Neal St; ⊖ Covent Garden
Etched brewery mirrors, red ceiling, mahogany furniture, some partitioned booths, lots of old local prints; popular lunchtime food from separate side counter, friendly staff, three well kept McMullens ales; piped music, games machine, often crowded; open all day

130. OPERA TAVERN
Catherine St, opposite Theatre Royal; ⊖ Covent Garden
Cheerful bare-boards pub, not too touristy, real ales such as Adnams, Fullers London Pride and Tetleys, reasonably priced snacks from sandwiches and baked potatoes up

131. PORTERHOUSE
Maiden Lane; ⊖/≋ Charing Cross
London outpost of Dublin's Porterhouse microbrewery; shiny three-level maze of stairs, galleries and copper ducting and piping, some nice design touches; their own interesting if pricy unpasteurised draught beers inc Porter and two Stouts (they do a comprehensive tasting tray), also their TSB real ale and a guest, lots of bottled beers, good choice of wines by the glass, reasonably priced food 12-9 from soup and open sandwiches up, with some emphasis on rock oysters; sonorous openwork clock, neatly cased bottled beer displays; piped music, irish bands Weds-Fri and Sun, big-screen sports TV (repeated in gents'); open all day, tables on front terrace

132. SALISBURY
St Martins Lane; ⊖ Leicester Square
Floridly Victorian with plenty of atmosphere, theatrical sweeps of red velvet, huge sparkling mirrors and cut and etched glass, glossy brass and mahogany; wide food choice from simple snacks to long-running smoked salmon lunches and salad bar (even doing Sun lunches over Christmas and New Year); well kept real ales such as Broughton Ghillie, Courage Directors, Fullers London Pride, Charles Wells Bombardier and Youngs Special, decent house wines, friendly service; no smoking back room

133. SHERLOCK HOLMES
Northumberland St; aka Northumberland Arms;
⊖ Embankment
Particularly fine collection of Holmes memorabilia, inc complete model of his apartment, also silent videos of black and white Holmes films; Boddingtons, Flowers IPA, Fullers London Pride and Wadworths 6X, usual furnishings, lunchtime pub food from doorstep sandwiches up; young staff, upstairs restaurant; busy lunchtime

134. SHIP
Gate St; ⊖ Holborn
Interesting bare-boards corner pub in narrow alley, with painted plaster relief ceiling and upstairs overflow, well kept ales such as Greene King Old Speckled Hen, Theakstons and Charles Wells Bombardier, usual food, friendly service; popular at lunchtime

135. SHIP & SHOVELL
Craven Passage, off Craven St; ⊖/≋ Charing Cross
Under Charing Cross station, with four Badger real ales kept well, reasonably priced food, welcoming service and civilised atmosphere; warm fire, bright lighting, pleasant décor inc interesting prints, mainly naval (to support a fanciful connection between this former coal-heavers' pub properly called Ship & Shovel with Sir Cloudesley Shovell, the early 18th-c admiral), cosy back section; TV

136. TAPPIT HEN
William IV St; ⊖/≋ Charing Cross
Typical of a long-standing (mainly London) chain of dependable bars run by Davys the wine merchants; splendid range of wines by the glass, a real ale named Old Wallop which tastes not unlike Bass, good coffee (free refills), decent bar food all day from good sandwiches and sharing plates to a few hot dishes (most people

come for the food – this one also has a lunchtime and evening restaurant menu), neat and friendly service; comfortable bentwood chairs around cast-iron framed tables on distressed boards around the L-shaped bar, more up a step or two by the street windows, some panelling; a few traditional tavern touches – though the style is now more clean-cut and up-to-date than it used to be; open all day

137. WELSH HARP
Chandos Pl; ⊖/⇌ Charing Cross

Unpretentious pub with some interesting if not always well executed portraits on its red walls, lovely front stained glass, congenial seating layout with nice high benches around back tables and along wall counter; unusual ales such as Elgoods, Harveys and York, friendly welcome

NORTH LONDON

138. CHAPEL
Penton Street, N1; ⊖ Angel

It's a shame this cosy bar isn't open all day or even a long lunchtime, but admittedly the décor and certainly the style and atmosphere of the place suit its evening-only hours to a T. The ecclesiastical theme runs to red and black wall lamps on partly panelled whitewashed walls, an ornate stone-effect bar counter, and stained-glass doors. One of the glass-topped tables, which have red candle-holders, is made from an intricately carved church door. Pretty white fairy lights decorate the bar, window frames and brick arches. One of the arches leads down to a dance floor with a frequently used DJ box in a pulpit, red spotlights and overhead mural. Comfortable brown leather chairs push together to form a huge settee on a low platform to the right of the bar; elsewhere is a comfortable mix of leather chairs, settees and padded bar stools. They also have an upstairs restaurant, and a heated roof terrace. The lavatories are very much in keeping.

Bar food (Sun lunchtime only) ~ (020) 7833 4090 ~ DJs, live music and entertainment Fri-Sun ~ Open 12-2, 5-11 (12 Thurs, 2am Fri and Sat); 12-11 Sun; cl Mon-Weds lunchtime

139. COMPTON ARMS

Compton Avenue, off Canonbury Road, N1; ⊖ Highbury & Islington

Hidden away up a peaceful mews, this well run tiny local has the unexpected bonus of a very pleasant crazy-paved terrace behind, with benches and tables among flowers under a big sycamore tree; there may be heaters in winter, and occasional barbecues in summer. Inside, the unpretentious low-ceilinged rooms are simply furnished with wooden settles and assorted stools and chairs, with local pictures on the walls; it has a very appealing village-local feel, and though there is a TV and piped music, the only games are things like chess, Jenga and Battleships. Well kept Greene King Abbot, IPA and Ruddles and a weekly changing guest on handpump, and around a dozen wines by the glass; friendly service. Good value bar food such as baguettes, and seven different types of sausage served with mashed potato and home-made red onion gravy (£4.95); their Sunday roasts come in two sizes, normal (£4.45) and large (£5.95). The pub is deep in Arsenal country, so can get busy on match days.

Bar food (12-2.30, 6-8.30; 12-4 Sat and Sun) ~ (020) 7359 6883 ~ Children welcome in family room till 8pm ~ Open 12-11(10.30 Sun)

140. DRAPERS ARMS
Barnsbury Street, N1; ⊖ Highbury & Islington

Good food is the draw at this made-over big-windowed early 19th-c pub in its quiet residential street: the choice might include steamed mussels with cider and bacon (£5/£9.50 as a main course), toasted ham and cheese sandwich or pitta with hummus, carrot, coriander and spinach (£5.20), home-made burger with guacamole and blue cheese (£7.50), liver and bacon (£13), coq au vin (£13.50) and rib of beef with sauce béarnaise (£15.50); the puddings (all £5) include a first-class sticky toffee. Everything tastes really fresh, with clean, carefully judged flavours and tempting presentation; service is good, helpful and unobtrusive. Big colourful bunches of flowers, inset shelves of paperbacks and board games, and a couple of groups of settees and armchairs, offset what might otherwise seem rather a severe open-plan layout and décor, with high-backed dining chairs or booths on dark bare boards, high ceilings, a few big drapery prints on dusky pink walls, and a pair of large fireplaces and mirrors precisely facing each other across the front area. The choice of wines by the glass (including champagne) is first rate, and they have Courage Best and Greene King Old Speckled Hen on handpump. On our inspection visit they had piped jazz and swing.

Bar food (12-3, 7-10.30; not Sun evening) ~ (020) 7619 0348 ~ Children welcome till 8pm ~ Open 11-11; 12-10.30 Sun; cl 24-27 Dec, 1-2 Jan

141. DUKE OF CAMBRIDGE

St Peters Street, N1; ⊖ Angel, though some distance away

This well refurbished corner house was London's first completely organic pub, with an excellent range of impeccably sourced drinks and food. Prices for both are perhaps higher than you'd pay for a non-organic meal, but it's usually worth the extra to enjoy choices and flavours you won't find anywhere else. Changing twice a day, the blackboard menu might include things like pumpkin, pear and celery soup (£4.50), bruschetta with chicken livers, dandelion leaves, sherry and crème fraîche (£6), roasted vegetables with parmesan and hazelnut crust (£9), bacon-wrapped scallops with tartare potato cake and basil crème (£10.50), fried red mullet with linguine, lemon and chilli sauce (£12), home-smoked lamb fillet with potato, aubergine and feta gratin (£13), and white chocolate and berry cheesecake (£4.50); children's helpings. A note explains that though they do all they can to ensure their game and fish have been sourced from suppliers using sustainable methods, these can't officially be classed as organic. They make all their own bread, pickles, ice-cream and so on. On handpump are four organic real ales: from London's small Pitfield Brewery Eco Warrior and Singhboulton (named for the pub's two owners), St Peters Best, and a guest such as East Kent Goldings or Shoreditch Organic Stout. They also have organic draught lagers and cider, organic spirits, and a very wide range of organic wines, many of which are available by the glass; we haven't yet personally verified the claim that organic drinks are less likely to cause a hangover. The full range of drinks is chalked on a blackboard, and also includes good coffees and teas, and a spicy ginger ale. The big, busy main room is simply decorated and furnished, with lots of chunky wooden tables, pews and benches on bare boards, a couple of big metal vases with colourful flowers, daily papers, and carefully positioned soft lighting around the otherwise bare walls. The atmosphere is warmly inviting, with the constant sound of civilised chat from a steady stream of varied customers; no music or games machines. A corridor leads off past a few tables and an open kitchen to a couple of smaller candlelit rooms, more formally set for eating; there's also a small side terrace. Some areas are no smoking. A couple of recent reports have detected a slight dip in the usual high standards, which we hope was only temporary. The licensees run the Crown in Victoria Park (see entry 283) along similar lines.

Bar food (12.30-3(3.30 Sat and Sun), 6.30-10.30(10 Sun))
~ Restaurant ~ (020) 7359 3066 ~ Children welcome ~
Dogs allowed in bar ~ Open 12-11(10.30 Sun);
cl 25-26 Dec

142. HOUSE
Canonbury Road, N1; ⊖ Highbury & Islington

The trend for transforming once-neglected London locals has become almost formulaic, so it's always exciting to find one that sets new standards – which this refurbished brick house does in spades. That its food has become so highly regarded so quickly isn't entirely surprising: the chef won top gourmet points for his cooking at Quo Vadis, and he's brought the same sure-handed approach to the House. But it isn't simply the meals that impress; as much thought has been put into the look and feel of the place, from the bespoke tables and carefully crafted wood to the art deco-influenced central bar counter, with mirrored panels in the centre and unusual chairs all around. It's essentially open plan, big, but cosy, with a couple of very comfortable areas based around the two brick fireplaces (the only original features left); sofas, newspapers and style mags make these corners feel almost homely. There are ceiling fans throughout, and the overall impression is rather like an elegant blend of local pub, trendy bar and smart restaurant. Most people eat in the dining area at the back, but there are plenty of tables elsewhere – and you can choose from the same menu at any of them. A typical choice might include soup (£5.50), tatin of red onion with grilled goats cheese (£5.95), parfait of foie gras, chicken livers and armagnac with toasted brioche (£6.95), cottage pie (£12.50), barbary duck leg confit with pommes anna, braised cabbage and bitter-sweet jus (£13.50), crab spaghettini with chilli, lemon and parsley (£13.95), roast corn-fed chicken, lemon and thyme confit and artichoke risotto (£14), and calves liver bourguignonne (£14.50); at lunchtime and between 5.30 and 6.30 they do a set menu, with two courses for £12.95, and three for £14.95. It may be worth booking at busy times. Part of the restaurant is no smoking. There's a good range of drinks, including a wide choice of wines, Adnams Broadside (not cheap, even for London), quite a selection of teas and hot drinks, and, if you're really pushing the boat out, a trolley of post-prandial liqueurs. Smiling, friendly service; piped music. A terrace in front has tables overlooking the road.

Bar food (12-2.30(3.30 wknds; not Mon lunch),
6.30-10.30) ~ Restaurant ~ (020) 7704 7410 ~ Children
welcome ~ Open 11-11; cl Mon till 5pm

143. WATERSIDE
York Way, N1; ⊖/≥ Kings Cross
A useful place to know if passing through Kings Cross, this handily placed pub benefits from an unexpectedly relaxing outside terrace overlooking the Battlebridge Basin, usually busy with boats. Heaters keep it pleasant all year round. The building is a nicely done pastiche of a 17th-c cider barn, with stripped brickwork, latticed windows, genuinely old stripped timbers in white plaster, lots of dimly lit alcoves, spinning wheels, milkmaids' yokes, and horsebrasses and so on, with plenty of rustic tables and wooden benches. Adnams, Fullers London Pride and a changing guest such as Charles Wells Bombardier on handpump, with cocktails in summer and mulled wine in winter. Bar food (served all day exc Sun) has an emphasis on fairly formidable pizzas (from £4.95), though they also do sandwiches (from £3.25), and hot dishes

like fish pie (£5.45), and mushroom ravioli with four-cheese sauce or steak in red wine (£5.95); they have a two-for-one meal offer Mon-Thurs. Live jazz Weds evenings. Pool, fruit machine, and sometimes loudish jukebox.
Bar food (12-9; 12-4.30 Sun) ~ (020) 7713 8613 ~
Children in eating area of bar ~ Live jazz Weds evenings ~
Open 11-11; 12-11 Sat; 12-10.30 Sun; cl 25-26 Dec,
1 Jan

144. ALBION
Thornhill Rd; ⊖ Angel
Cosy local feel in several distinct traditional areas rambling around central bar, old prints and soft lighting (some gas lamps), small comfortable no smoking back restaurant area (front can get a bit smoky); reasonably priced straightforward food from sandwiches and baked potatoes to plenty of specials, well kept Fullers London Pride and changing guest beers such as Coniston Bluebird and Mordue Workie Ticket; interesting Victorian gents' piped music, TV, fruit machine, games machine; flower-decked railed front courtyard, big heated back terrace with lots of close-set tables under huge parasol, weeping willow and vine bower

145. BARNSBURY
Liverpool Rd; ⊖ Highbury & Islington
New food pub, stripped back to original woodwork and fireplaces, with contemporary art for sale, wines inc organic ones, real ales and belgian beers; food all day Sun

146. BIERODROME
Upper St; ⊖ Highbury & Islington
Five belgian beers on tap (they do taster trays) from stainless-steel servery, lots of bottled ones, plenty of genevers and other interesting spirits, eight wines by the glass, cocktails (by the jug if you want); big windows at the front, seating inc some booths with leatherette banquettes around dark modern tables, stretching back into darker ply-panelled vaulted tunnels, the one on the right set as a café; wide food choice from cheese croquettes or bitterballen through moules to fishcakes and burgers; well reproduced piped 1970s pop music; one of a small chain, usually in areas busy at night

147. CAMDEN HEAD
Camden Walk; ⊖ Angel
Reliable standby, very handy for the antiques market, enjoyable food inc good specials; tables outside

148. CROWN
Cloudesley Rd; ⊖ Angel
Good food and atmosphere in gastro-pub with helpful, friendly staff and fashionably distressed look – stripped old tables and so forth

149. ELBOW ROOM
Chapel Market; ⊖ Angel
Huge sprawling modern pool hall, part of a small chain with branches in Shoreditch and Westbourne Grove (also Leeds and Bristol); purple pool tables (£6-£9 an hour, £10 deposit), with globe-lit red and cream leather booths and banquettes divided by light wood-effect pillars, industrial-look red leather bar stools and tables, and lots of standing space in front of the colourfully lit bar counter; dark ceiling, with a bright variety of mirror-panelled walls and lots of

shiny blond wood; lagers on tap and cocktails, with snack food such as nachos, club sandwiches and burgers; popular with a young crowd, especially at wknds, piped pop and music videos, frequent DJs and live music

150. JORENE CELESTE
Upper St; ⊖ Highbury & Islington
Stretching far back from a charming small bow-windowed façade, long boards accentuating its length, lots of heavily gilt mirrors and late 19th-c pictures, fresh flowers on heavy tables (good mix of sizes), some soft blue or beige settees, and potted palms; food with middle eastern leanings

151. KINGS HEAD
Upper St; ⊖ Angel
Green décor and large mirrors in big-windowed high-ceilinged Victorian pub in a good spot; well kept Adnams, Tetleys and Wadworths 6X from horseshoe bar with fine old cash register, hot solid-fuel fires, theatre lighting, even some pensioned-off row seats, and lots of dated theatre photographs; bar food (via ancient dumb waiter) and popular bistro, decent coffee; an oasis of calm on wkdy lunchtimes, can get packed wknds; singer most nights, good theatre in back room (but hard seats there)

152. NARROW BOAT
St Peters St; ⊖ Angel
Handy for central Islington but quietly placed, with window tables overlooking the Regent's Canal in light and airy bar; yellow walls over dark dado, also tall bar stools and a settee, big open fire, national flags; boat décor in end extension (opened up to white steamer rails on warm days); wide range of usual blackboard food

(all day Sat, not Sun evening), Youngs and other real ales, and good summer jugs of Pimm's; fruit machine, jukebox, big-screen sports TV, quiz night Sun, music

153. WENLOCK ARMS
Wenlock Rd; ⊖ Old Street
Plain and popular open-plan local in a bleak bit of London; warmly welcoming service, central bar serving ten or so well kept changing ales from small breweries, always inc a Mild; also farm cider and perry, foreign bottled beers, snacks inc good salt beef sandwiches; alcove seating, piano in pride of place, coal fires, darts; piped music; open all day; modern jazz Tues, trad Fri, piano Sun lunch

N4 (Finsbury Park)

154. FALTERING FULLBACK
Perth Rd/Ennis Rd; ⊖ Finsbury Park
Comfortable small corner pub, two softly lit bars, friendly staff and locals; well kept Fullers London Pride, lunchtime bar food; may be quiet piped music, silenced sports TV; nice outside area

155. SALISBURY
Grand Parade, Green Lanes; ⇌ Harringay Green Lanes
Grandiose late-Victorian former hotel, reopened after careful refurbishment of its spacious richly ornamented bars; dark velvet, leather and mahogany, intricate tiling and mirrors, well kept ales such as Fullers London Pride and Ridleys Old Bob, food in bar and dining room (not Sun evening); open all day, till 1am Thurs-Sat

N6 (Highgate)

156. FLASK
Highgate West Hill; ⊖ Highgate
Comfortable Georgian pub, mostly modernised but still has intriguing up-and-down layout, sash-windowed bar hatch, panelling and high-backed carved settle tucked away in snug lower area (but this nice original core open only wknds and summer); decent all-day food (limited Sun) inc salad bar, changing beers such as Adnams and Harveys, friendly service; very busy Sat lunchtime, well behaved children allowed, close-set picnic-sets out in attractive heated front courtyard; handy for strolls around Highgate village or Hampstead Heath

N12 (Finchley)

157. TALLY HO
High Rd, North Finchley; ⊖ Woodside Park
Imposing landmark pub comfortably reworked, with old local photographs, good value all-day food and beer, and large upstairs no smoking room allowing children if eating

N13 (Palmers Green)

158. WISHING WELL
Aldermans Hill; ⇌ Palmers Green
Friendly irish pub with plenty of atmosphere, perhaps even free drinks on a Sat if an Irish Lottery winner is celebrating here; frequent irish live music

N20 (Totteridge)

159. ORANGE TREE
Totteridge; ⊖ Totteridge & Whetstone
Rambling Vintage Inn, good value standard food from sandwiches to
fish served efficiently even on busy wknds (good Sun roasts); well
kept Bass and Fullers London Pride, fine choice of wines by the glass,
freshly squeezed orange juice and coffee; friendly staff, light and
airy décor with inglenook log fires; welcoming to children (and
walkers, who leave boots in porch); tables out in pleasant
surroundings by duckpond – still has a village feel

NW1 (Marylebone)

160. CHAPEL
Chapel Street, NW1; ⊖ Edgware Road
Very good, well served and presented food continues to be
the hallmark of this much-modernised child-friendly gastro-
pub. The menu changes every day, but might include soups
such as cream of pumpkin, tomato and cumin (£3.50) or
jamaican chicken and banana (£4), brie, olive and pimientos
tartlet (£4.50), ragout of smoked tuna, trout and eel with
capers and sun-dried tomato (£5), asparagus tortelli with
basil, tomato and gruyère cheese (£8.50), pan-fried calves
liver with parma ham, port, mash and rosemary (£11.50),
maltese-style braised lamb shank with sweet potato (£12.50),
seared swordfish steak with celeriac, potato gratin, lemon

and butter sauce (£13), and puddings like chocolate and banana crème brûlée (£3.50). Prompt, charming service from friendly staff, who may bring delicious warm walnut bread to your table while you're waiting. The atmosphere is always cosmopolitan – perhaps more relaxed and civilised at lunchtime, then altogether busier and louder in the evenings. Light and spacious, the cream-painted main room is dominated by the open kitchen; furnishings are smart but simple, with plenty of plain wooden tables around the bar, and more in a side room with a big fireplace. It can fill up quite quickly, so you may have to wait to eat during busier periods. There are more tables on a terrace outside, popular with chic local office workers on fine lunchtimes. Well kept Adnams and Greene King IPA on handpump (both rather expensive, even for London), a good range of interesting wines (up to half by the glass), cappuccino and espresso, fresh orange juice, and a choice of tisanes such as peppermint or strawberry and vanilla. In the evening, trade is more evenly split between diners and drinkers, and the music can be quite noticeable then, especially at weekends.
Bar food (12-2.30, 7-10) ~ (020) 7402 9220 ~ Children welcome ~ Dogs welcome ~ Open 12-11(10.30 Sun); cl some bank hols

161. ENGINEER

Gloucester Avenue, NW1; ⊖ Chalk Farm or Camden Town

Handy for Regent's Canal (and once linked to it by underground tunnels), this friendly well established food pub is said to have been named after Brunel, who's thought to have built it; another theory has the handsome Victorian building's architect as Robert Stevenson. What's especially nice about it is that although there's an emphasis on the very good food, it's by no means simply a gastro-pub: drinkers are made very welcome in the simply furnished little bar. Altogether cosier than the Lansdowne just up the road (see next page), it has stripped wooden floors, chunky wooden tables with lit candles, and a comfortably civilised feel; there are newspapers and flowers on the curved wooden counter, mirrors on the wall, fairy lights around a window into the kitchen, and a small TV in the corner; piped music. Well kept Adnams Broadside and Fullers London Pride on handpump, a short list of cocktails, and a good choice of wines by the glass. You can eat in here or in the appealing adjacent restaurant, which has changing displays of contemporary art or photographs. A busy day in the kitchen starts with their very popular breakfasts (they do a good range of smoothies), then moves on to a wider menu that might include soup with home-made bread (£4), corn and white chocolate tamales (steamed corn cakes) with blackened tomato salsa (£6.25), baked figs stuffed with mozzarella wrapped in serrano ham (£7.95), and main courses such as salmon fishcakes with coriander, chilli and ginger (£9.55), beer-battered plaice with minted mushy peas (£10.50), spiced polenta stack with grilled piquillo peppers, spinach and mushroom ragout (£11.25), crispy baby chicken braised with soy and ginger with bok choi, basmati rice and caramelised chilli sauce (£14), and organic rib-eye steak with roast red onions, garlic mushrooms and horseradish butter (£16.50); all their meats are free-range or organic, and they do very good fish specials. They're kind to children, with a separate menu and maybe crayons (you'll probably need to fold away pushchairs). A highlight in summer is the very pleasant garden, where olive trees may be festooned with pretend kumquats or other fanciful additions.

Bar food (all day) ~ Restaurant ~ (020) 7722 0950 ~ Children welcome ~ Dogs allowed in bar ~ Open 9-11

162. LANSDOWNE

Gloucester Avenue, NW1; ⊖ Chalk Farm or Camden Town

From the outside it looks like a slightly scruffy local, but don't be fooled: this big buzzing gastro-pub is an excellent choice for a good, thoughtfully prepared meal. You're made very welcome if you've come for just a drink, but the food is very much the focus: blackboards listing their snacks and meals are everywhere, and you can get something to eat pretty much all day. They do good pizzas until early evening (around £8), with the fuller menu typically including things like spiced spinach soup (£4.20), half a dozen rock oysters

(£8.50), linguine with chilli, garlic, mozzarella and fresh basil (£8), organic chicken stew with butternut squash, orange and savoy cabbage (£10.50), smoked haddock with black treacle bacon, fried pink fir apple potatoes, and an egg, caper and endive salad (£12.50), and Black Mountain rib-eye steak (£14.50). Everything is home-made (including their bread, sizeable chips, and ice-cream), and they do a nice range of bar snacks such as anchovies or caper berries and peppers. The open-plan, L-shaped room has plenty of space to absorb the nicely varied mix of customers, and is simply but smartly decorated and furnished, with wooden floorboards and good-sized tables, cream and black paintwork, a couple of sofas, a big, colourful modern painting, and flowers and newspapers around a central standing pillar. The busy kitchen opens off, and stairs lead up to the elegant restaurant. Well kept Fullers London Pride and Woodfordes Wherry on handpump, and an extensive wine list; good friendly service; no music or machines. They're very dog- and child-friendly; at lunchtimes it's quite a favourite with groups of new mothers. There are a few tables outside. *Bar food (12.30-3(4 Sat; not Mon lunch), 7-10(9.30 Sun)) ~ Restaurant ~ (020) 7483 0409 ~ Children welcome ~ Open 12-11; 12-10.30 Sun; cl Mon till 6pm*

163. GLOBE

Marylebone Rd; ⊖ Baker Street

Handsome and neatly kept L-shaped pubby bar, good variety of
intimate seating on polished boards, real ales such as Courage Best
and Directors, Ridleys Rumpus, Charles Wells Bombardier and
Youngs Special, foreign bottled beers; sensibly priced food from
baked potatoes up; seats outside (a mass of flowers in summer),
handy for Mme Tussauds

164. HEAD OF STEAM

Eversholt St; ⊖/≷ Euston

Large, well worn in, Victorian-look bar up stairs from bus terminus
and overlooking it, lots of railway nameplates, other memorabilia
and enthusiast magazines for sale, also Corgi collection, unusual
model trains and buses; nine interesting well kept ales (also take-
away) changing from session to session, most from little-known small
breweries, monthly themed beer festivals, Weston's farm cider and
perry, lots of bottled beers and vodkas; kind service, simple cheap
bar lunches, no smoking area, downstairs restaurant; TV, bar
billiards, games machine, security-coded basement lavatories; open
all day

165. METROPOLITAN

Baker Street Station, Marylebone Rd; ⊖ Baker Street

Cool and elegant showpiece Wetherspoons in ornate Victorian hall,
lots of tables on one side, very long bar the other; their usual good
beer choice and prices, no smoking areas, lack of piped music and
so forth

166. ROYAL GEORGE
Eversholt St; ⊖/≥ Euston
Roomy and tidily kept, with well kept beers and enjoyable cheap food inc bargains for two

NW3 (Hampstead)

167. FLASK
Flask Walk, NW3; ⊖ Hampstead
Its name a reminder of the days when the pub distributed mineral water from Hampstead's springs, this properly old-fashioned local is still a popular haunt of Hampstead artists, actors and characters. The snuggest and most individual part is the cosy lounge at the front, with plush green seats and banquettes curving round the panelled walls, a unique Victorian screen dividing it from the public bar, an attractive fireplace, and a very laid-back and rather villagey atmosphere. A comfortable orange-lit room with period prints and a few further tables leads into a rather smart dining conservatory which, with its plants, prominent wine bottles and neat table linen, feels a bit like a wine bar. A couple of white iron tables are squeezed into the tiny back yard. Particularly well kept Youngs Bitter, Special and seasonal brews on handpump, around 20 wines by the glass, and decent coffees – they have a machine that grinds the beans to order. Bar food might include sandwiches (from

£2.50), soup, and daily changing specials like chicken casserole, lamb curry or spiced minced beef pie with a cheese and leek mash topping (from £5.50); they do fish and chips at weekends. A plainer public bar (which you can get into only from the street) has leatherette seating, cribbage, backgammon, lots of space for darts, fruit machines, trivia, and big-screen SkyTV. Friendly service from sociable young staff. There are quite a few tables out in the alley.
Bar food (12-3(4 Sun), 6-8.30; not Sun or Mon evening) ~ Restaurant ~ (020) 7435 4580 ~ Children in eating area of bar and restaurant ~ Dogs allowed in bar ~ Open 11-11; 12-10.30 Sun

168. HOLLY BUSH
Holly Mount, NW3; ⊖ Hampstead

A characterful and civilised spot, this cheery Hampstead local is these days winning fans not just for its atmosphere and timeless style, but for its beers and above average food. It's perhaps especially appealing in the evenings, when a good mix of chatty locals and visitors fills the old-fashioned and individual front bar. Under the dark sagging ceiling are brown and cream panelled walls (decorated with old advertisements and a few hanging plates), open fires, bare boards, and cosy bays formed by partly glazed partitions. Slightly more intimate, the back room, named after the painter George Romney, has an embossed red ceiling, panelled and etched glass alcoves, and ochre-painted brick walls covered with small prints; piped music, darts. Well kept Adnams Bitter and Broadside, Fullers London Pride, Harveys Sussex and an unusual guest like Hydes Hubble Bubble on handpump, some unusual bottled beers, plenty of whiskies, and a good wine list; friendly service. Bar food includes soup (£3.50), welsh rarebit (£5), pies like beef and ale or carrot, parsnip, celeriac and cider (from £8), various sausages with cheddar mash and gravy (£8.50), slow roast lamb shank (£9.50), and roasted free-range chicken in smoked paprika sauce (£10), Guinness and mushroom pie (£8.75). An upstairs area is no smoking at weekends. There are tables on the pavement outside. The pub is reached by a delightful stroll along some of Hampstead's most villagey streets.

Bar food (12.30-4, 6.30-10; 12.30-8.30 Sun; not Mon lunchtime) ~ Restaurant ~ (020) 7435 2892 ~ Children welcome ~ Dogs allowed in bar ~ Open 12-11(10.30 Sun)

169. OLDE WHITE BEAR
Well Road, NW3; ⊖ Hampstead

Very close to the heath, this neo-Victorian pub is a notably friendly place that attracts a wonderfully diverse mix of people of all ages. The dimly lit knocked-through bar has three separate-seeming areas: the biggest has lots of Victorian prints and cartoons on the walls, as well as wooden stools, cushioned captain's chairs, a couple of big tasselled armchairs, a flowery sofa, a handsome fireplace and an

ornate Edwardian sideboard. A brighter section at the end
has elaborate brocaded pews and wooden Venetian blinds,
while a central area has Lloyd Loom furniture, dried flower
arrangements and signed photographs of actors and
playwrights. Bar food is served all day, from a range
including soup (£3.50), good elaborate sandwiches (from
£4), ploughman's, japanese tempura prawns or chicken
satay (£5), a daily pasta dish (£5.75), pork and leek
sausages or thai chicken curry (£6.50), cod in beer batter or
beef and Guinness pie (£7), and sirloin steak (£9.50);
Sunday roasts. Adnams, Greene King Abbot, Fullers London
Pride and Youngs on handpump. There are a few tables in
front, and more in a courtyard behind. Soft piped music,
cards, chess, TV, and excellent Thursday quiz nights. Parking
may be a problem at times – it's mostly residents' permits
only nearby (there are no restrictions on Sundays).
*Bar food (12-9) ~ (020) 7435 3758 ~ Children welcome ~
Dogs allowed in bar ~ Open 11-11; 12-11 Sat; 12-10.30
Sun*

170. SPANIARDS INN

**Spaniards Lane, NW3; ⊖ Hampstead, but some distance
away, or from Golders Green station take 220 bus**
Tales of ghosts and highwaymen help draw the crowds to this
busy former toll house, but to our mind the highlight is
perhaps its charming garden, said to be where Keats wrote
'Ode to a Nightingale' in 1820. Nicely arranged in a series

of areas separated by judicious planting of shrubs, it has slatted wooden tables and chairs on a crazy-paved terrace opening on to a flagstoned walk around a small lawn, with roses, a side arbour of wisteria and clematis, and an aviary. You may need to move fast to bag a table out here in summer. Inside, the low-ceilinged oak-panelled rooms of the attractive main bar have open fires, genuinely antique winged settles, candle-shaped lamps in shades, and snug little alcoves. Well kept Adnams, Fullers London Pride, Rebellion IPA and a seasonal guest like Hopback Summer Lightning on handpump – though in summer you might find the most popular drink is their big jug of Pimm's; newspapers, fruit machine. Under the new manager food is served all day, from a menu including ciabattas (from £4.95), soup (£3.95), greek salad or spaghetti meatballs in tomato sauce (£6.50), mushroom, parmesan and lemon risotto (£6.95), home-made pork, garlic and herb sausages (£7.50), and steak and kidney pudding (£7.95); they do a paella on Saturdays (£7.50), and a roast on Sundays. The food bar is no smoking at lunchtimes; upstairs, the Georgian Turpin Room is no smoking all day. The pub is believed to have been named after the Spanish ambassador to the court of James I, who had a private residence here. It's fairly handy for Kenwood, and indeed during the 1780 Gordon Riots the then landlord helped save the house from possible disaster, cunningly giving so much free drink to the mob on its way to burn it down that by the time the Horse Guards arrived the rioters were lying drunk and incapable on the floor. Parking can be difficult – especially when people park here to walk their dogs on the heath.

Bar food (12-10) ~ (020) 8731 6571 ~ Children welcome ~ Dogs allowed in bar ~ Open 11-11; 12-10.30 Sun

171. DUKE OF HAMILTON
New End; ⊖ Hampstead

Attractive family-run Fullers local, good value, with good range of seating, well kept London Pride, ESB and a seasonal beer, also Biddenden farm cider; open all day, suntrap terrace; next to New End Theatre

172. ENTERPRISE
Haverstock Hill; ⊖ Chalk Farm

Enjoyably unpretentious and welcoming, with muted irish theme (Flann O'Brien on the glass of the main doors, pictures of irish literati inside), friendly efficient service, well kept beer, daily papers; comedy nights upstairs (usually Weds), occasional live music there, very busy Fri night; open all day

173. OLD BULL & BUSH
North End Way; ⊖ Golders Green

Attractive Victorian pub, quiet on wkdy lunchtimes, with comfortable sofa and easy chairs, nooks and crannies, side library bar with lots of bookshelves and pictures and mementoes of Florrie Ford whose song made the pub famous; enjoyable bar food inc filled bagels and good Sun specials, reasonable prices, decent wines, restaurant with no smoking area; in the evening piped music may be loud, with trendy lighting; good provision for families, pleasant terrace

NW5 (Kentish Town)

174. TORRIANO
Torriano Ave; ⊖ Kentish Town
Popular with local musicians and creatives, unusual range of cocktails and interesting wines as well as lagers and real ale, lunchtime panini and home-made soup, occasional live music wknds; tables in convivial back yard

NW6 (Queens Park)

175. SALUSBURY
Salusbury Road, NW6; ⊖ Queens Park
Feeling very much the focal point of the area, this excellent place is highly regarded for its food but is just as appealing to drinkers, with the central servery more or less the dividing line between the smarter dining room and the bustling bar. Both sides fill up fast, so if you're planning to eat, booking is recommended, especially at weekends. Served from an open kitchen, the meals aren't cheap, but they're splendid quality, from a mostly italian-influenced menu that might include roast lamb shank with shallots (£12), monkfish with speck and peppers (£14), and lobster brodetto with shellfish and

squid (£16.50); their bread is delicious, and the service friendly and knowledgeable. On Sundays the menu is based around a choice of roasts; they do a children's menu then. Relaxed and quietly cool, the bar is comfortable and chatty, with lots of packed-together tables, stripped wooden floors, standard lamps creating a very homely effect, and a mix of modern art, oversized photographs and classic 60s album covers on the half-panelled cream or red-painted walls. There are a good few mirrors, with many more in the dining room, which also has big, chunky wooden tables, careful spotlighting, and plenty of fresh flowers; piped music. Well kept Adnams and Bass or Greene King Old Speckled Hen on handpump, and a splendid wine list, with a dozen or more by the glass. Dogs on leads are welcome in the bar. There are tables out in front of the striking dark wood and glass exterior, under an awning. Next door is their own eclectically stocked deli, with lots of organic produce and some mouth-watering italian goodies. The success of both establishments has led to further expansion: as we went to press they were planning to open an adjacent pizzeria.

Bar food (12.30-3.30, 7-10.15) ~ Restaurant ~ (020) 7328 3286 ~ Children welcome till 7pm ~ Dogs allowed in bar ~ Open 12-11; closed Mon till 5pm

176. CORRIB REST
Salusbury Rd/Hopefield Ave; ⊖ Queens Park
Particularly friendly traditional irish pub, a real welcome for all, good disabled access and facilities; good value

177. LONG ROOM
Salusbury Rd; ⊖ Queens Park
Formerly the Montrose, huge comfortably refurbished bar with plenty of seats and space, very contemporary décor and styling, feels like a big chill-out lounge with comfortable sofas and laid-back music; long bar counter, and back open kitchen with pizzas from wood-fired oven and other dishes too; good coffee, fresh orange juice (open for breakfast), friendly staff; children most welcome

NW7 (Mill Hill)

178. RISING SUN
Marsh Lane/Highwood Hill; no nearby tube
Beautiful wisteria-covered local dating from 17th c, doing well under current tenants; small well restored main bar and atmospheric side snug on right with low ceilings, lots of dark panelling, timber and coal fires, big plainer lounge on left; well kept Adnams, Greene King Abbot, Youngs Special and occasional guest ales, good malt whiskies, enjoyable food from sandwiches to interesting hot dishes, polite and helpful well turned out staff; picnic-sets on pleasant back terrace, good walks nearby

NW8 (St Johns Wood)

179. CROCKERS
Aberdeen Pl; ⊖ Warwick Avenue
Magnificent original Victorian interior, full of showy marble, decorated plaster and opulent woodwork; relaxing and comfortable, with well kept Brakspears and Greene King, friendly service, decent food inc good Sun roasts; tables outside

180. DON PEPE
Frampton St; ⊖ Edgware Road
Engaging little bit of transplanted Spain, very relaxed atmosphere; stools at small bar counter with lively sports talk (spanish-channel TV up in one corner), good spanish house wines and friendly long-serving black-waistcoated staff; knobbed chairs at small dark varnished tables set for the wide choice of very reasonably priced authentic tapas (the mixed platter at £6.50 makes a cheap light lunch for two), white brick tile floor, plenty of varnished timbering, wrought iron, plastic flowers, and diplomas, photographs and cuttings on the swirly plaster; piped spanish music, live nights, restaurant

181. LORDS TAVERN
St Johns Wood Rd; ⊖ St Johns Wood
Next to Lords Cricket Ground, good range of food with thai flavours, well kept real ales, decent wine choice and friendly service; tables outside

SOUTH LONDON

182. ANCHOR

Park Street – Bankside, SE1; Southwark Bridge end; ⊖/≹
London Bridge

The wooden tables on the busy terrace of this old riverside pub offer unrivalled views of the Thames and the City. It's ideally placed for visits to the Tate Modern and the Globe Theatre, and happily an almost total, recent refurbishment hasn't overly affected the pub's character or appeal. The current building dates back to about 1750, when it was built to replace an earlier tavern, possibly the one that Pepys came to during the Great Fire of 1666. 'All over the Thames with one's face in the wind, you were almost burned with a shower of fire drops,' he wrote. 'When we could endure no more upon the water, we to a little ale-house on the Bankside and there staid till it was dark almost, and saw the fire grow.' It's a warren of dimly lit, creaky little rooms and passageways, with bare boards and beams, black panelling, old-fashioned high-backed settles, and sturdy leatherette chairs; even when it's invaded by tourists it's usually possible to retreat to one of the smaller rooms. Courage Best and Directors on handpump, as well as a dozen wines by the glass, jugs of Pimm's, mulled wine in winter, and various teas and coffees; two fruit machines, and occasionally rather loud piped music. Served all day, bar food includes filled

baguettes (from £4), and in the upstairs bar hot dishes such as fish and chips, home-baked pies and sausages and mash (£5.50); they do Sunday roasts. Parts of the bar and restaurant are no smoking (other areas can get smoky at times). Morris dancers occasionally pass by, and there are barbecues in summer. We have not yet heard from anyone staying in the new bedrooms, in a Premier Lodge behind.
Bar food (12-9) ~ Restaurant ~ (020) 7407 1577 ~
Children in restaurant and family room ~ Open 11-11;
12-10.30 Sun ~ Bedrooms: £78.25B/£84.50B

183. FIRE STATION
Waterloo Road, SE1; ⊖/≋ Waterloo
Very handy for the Old Vic and Waterloo Station, this bustling place is a splendid conversion of the former LCC central fire station. Popular with both diners and after-work drinkers, it's something of a cross between a warehouse and a schoolroom, with plenty of wooden pews, chairs and long tables (a few spilling on to the street), some mirrors and rather incongruous pieces of dressers, and brightly red-painted doors, shelves and modern hanging lightshades; the determinedly contemporary art round the walls is for sale, and there's a table with newspapers to read. It can get very noisy indeed in the evenings, which does add to the atmosphere – though if you're after a quiet drink you could find it overpowering. It's calmer at lunchtimes, and at weekends. Well kept Adnams Best, Charles Wells

Bombardier, Fullers London Pride, Shepherd Neame Spitfire and Youngs on handpump, as well as a number of bottled beers, variously flavoured teas, several malt whiskies, and a good choice of wines (a dozen by the glass). They serve a range of bar meals between 12 and 5.30, which might include several interestingly filled ciabattas and paninis (from £5.95), salads (from £6), and steamed mussels in coconut milk and thai spices (£10.95), but it's worth paying the extra to eat from the main menu, served from an open kitchen in the back dining room. Changing daily, this has things like baked pear and blue cheese tart with red onion potato salad (£9.95), roast duck breast with sweet potato wedges and sweet soya sauce or blackened kingfish with cornmeal fritters (£11.95), parsley-crusted calves liver with bacon and mustard mash (£12.50), and puddings such as peach and almond tart with custard sauce; some dishes can run out, so get there early for the best choice. They also do a set menu at lunchtimes and between 5.30 and 7, with two courses for £10.95, or three for £13.50. You can book tables. Piped modern jazz and other music fits into the good-natured hubbub; there's a TV for rugby matches. Several customers have recently found the service to be efficient rather than friendly – and one considered it to be neither.

Bar food (11-10; 12-9.15 Sun) ~ Restaurant ~
(020) 7620 2226 ~ Open 11-11; 12-10.30 Sun

184. FOUNDERS ARMS

Hopton Street (Bankside, SE1); ⊖ Blackfriars, and cross Blackfriars Bridge

Like a big, modern conservatory, this efficiently organised place benefits from one of the best settings of any pub along the Thames, particularly in the City, with fine views of the river, St Paul's, and the Millennium Bridge. Picnic-sets out on the big waterside terrace share the panorama. If you're inside, the lighting is nice and unobtrusive so that you can still see out across the river at night. Also handy for Shakespeare's Globe and the Tate Modern, it can get busy, particularly on weekday evenings, when it's popular with young City types for an after-work drink. Well kept Youngs Bitter, Special and seasonal brews from the modern bar counter angling along one side; also, coffee, tea and hot chocolate. Served pretty much all day, the enjoyable bar food includes sandwiches (from £3.95), paninis (from £4.75), soup (£3.95), sausages and mash (£7.45), fresh haddock in beer batter (£7.50), spinach and pumpkin curry (£7.85), steak and kidney pie (£8.45), and daily specials; Sunday roasts. Good, neat and cheerful service. One raised area is no smoking; piped music, and two fruit machines. Like many City pubs, it may close a little early on quieter nights. *Bar food (12-8.30(7 Sun)) ~ (020) 7928 1899 ~ Children in eating area of bar during food service ~ Open 11-11; 12-10.30 Sun*

185. GEORGE

off 77 Borough High Street, SE1; ⊖/⇌ Borough or London Bridge

Preserved by the National Trust, this splendid-looking place is probably the country's best example of a 17th-c coaching inn, but it isn't simply playing the heritage card; it's a proper, bustling pub, with a good atmosphere, friendly welcome, and a nice range of beers. Unless you know where you're going (or you're in one of the many tourist groups that flock here in summer) you may well miss it, as apart from the great gates there's little to indicate that such a gem still exists behind the less auspicious-looking buildings on the busy high street. The tiers of open galleries look down over a bustling cobbled courtyard with plenty of picnic-sets, and maybe Morris men and even Shakespeare in summer. Inside, the row of no-frills ground-floor rooms and bars all have square-latticed windows, black beams, bare floorboards, some panelling, plain oak or elm tables and old-fashioned built-in settles, along with a 1797 'Act of Parliament' clock, dimpled glass lantern-lamps and so forth. The snuggest refuge is the room nearest the street, where there's an ancient beer engine that looks like a cash register. Two rooms are no smoking at lunchtimes. In summer they open a bar with direct service into the courtyard. Well kept Bass, Fullers London Pride, Greene King Abbot, a beer brewed for the pub and a changing guest on handpump; mulled wine in winter, tea and coffee. Lunchtime bar food might include filled baked potatoes (from

£3), soup (£3.25), baguettes (from £3.50), ploughman's (£4.95), sausage and mash or roasted vegetable lasagne (£5.25), various salads (from £5.45), and steak, mushroom and Guinness pie (£5.45); evening meals in the restaurant are broadly similar, but a little more expensive. A splendid central staircase goes up to a series of dining rooms and to a gaslit balcony; darts, trivia. Their music nights can be quite jolly – anyone can join in the monthly cajun jam sessions. Incidentally, what survives today is only a third of what it once was; the building was 'mercilessly reduced', as E V Lucas put it, during the period when it was owned by the Great Northern Railway Company.

Bar food (12-3 (4 wknds)) ~ Restaurant ~ (020) 7407 2056 ~ Children welcome ~ Folk first Mon, Cajun third Mon ~ Open 11-11; 12-10.30 Sun

186. MARKET PORTER
Stoney Street, SE1; ⊖/≋ London Bridge

This busily pubby place has perhaps London's best range of real ales. They usually get through 20 different beers each week, with eight on at any one time. You'll always find Courage Best and Harveys Best, along with rapidly changing guests you're unlikely to have heard of before – let alone come across in this neck of the woods: our readers have recently enjoyed Archers Dublin Bay, Beowulf Bitter, Milk Street Beer, Skye Brevet Ale, and brews from the nearby London Bridge Brewery, all perfectly kept and served. The main part of the long U-shaped bar has rough wooden ceiling beams with beer barrels balanced on them, a heavy wooden bar counter with a beamed gantry, cushioned bar stools, an open fire, and 20s-style wall lamps. Sensibly priced, simple lunchtime bar food includes sandwiches (from £3.25), and paninis (£4.25), home-made pies and pasta (£5.95), and fish and chips wrapped in newspaper (£6.50); Sunday roasts. Obliging, friendly service; darts, fruit machine, TV and piped music. A cosy, partly panelled room has leaded glass windows and a couple of tables. The restaurant usually has an additional couple of real ales. They open between 6.30 and 8.30am for workers and porters from Borough Market. The company that own the pub, which can get a little full at lunchtimes although it's quiet in the afternoons, have various others around London; ones with similarly unusual beers (if not quite so many) can be found in Stamford Street and Seymour Place.

Bar food (12-3(5 Sat and Sun)) ~ Restaurant ~
(020) 7407 2495 ~ Open 6.30am-8.30am, then 11-11;
12-10.30 Sun

187. ROYAL OAK

Tabard Street, SE1; ⊖ Borough

This Victorian corner house has been transformed in the few years it's been owned by Sussex brewer Harveys. They've painstakingly re-created the look and feel of a traditional London alehouse so successfully, that you'd never imagine it wasn't like this all along. Despite being slightly off the beaten track, it can get very busy with a real mix of customers who've actively sought it out, partly for the chatty atmosphere, but also for the full range of impeccably kept Harveys beers, which you won't find anywhere else in town. Best-loved among these is perhaps their Sussex Best, but you'll also find their stronger Armada, as well as Mild, Pale Ale, and changing seasonal brews. Two small L-shaped rooms meander around the central wooden servery, which has a fine old clock in the middle. They're done out in a cosy, old-fashioned style: patterned rugs on the wooden floors, plates lined along a delft shelf, black and white scenes or period sheet music on the red-painted walls, and a good mix of wooden tables and chairs. It almost goes without saying, but there's no music or machines. Good honest bar food includes sausage and mash (£4.95), cod and chips (£5.25), and steak and ale pie or gammon and egg (£5.50). Note: the pub is closed at weekends.

Bar food (12-2.30, 6-9.15) ~ (020) 7357 7173 ~ Dogs welcome ~ Open 11.30-11; cl Sat and Sun

188. STUDIO SIX
Gabriels Wharf, SE1; ⊖/≈ Waterloo

In the heart of an appealing riverside assemblage of eclectic shops, restaurants and bars, this is a very popular place for a relaxed meal or drink, especially in summer, when the sheltered tables outside are packed with visitors and regulars enjoying the surrounding bustle. From the outside, the timber-framed building looks rather like a diner, but inside it feels more of a bistro, with stripped wooden floors and tables in the big main room, an attractive curved bar counter, and glass-panelled doors looking out on to the terrace. Boxes stacked on the beams create a cheerfully ramshackle effect, and there's a real buzz of conversation that easily drowns out the soft piped music. A smaller second room has black and white checked flooring, lots more tables packed close together, and a lighter air thanks to its frosted skylights. Big blackboards list the wide range of well priced meals, usually including things like spicy lentil soup (£3.50), sun-dried tomato and butternut squash risotto or caesar salad (£7.50), lamb chops with leek mash, bacon and rosemary jus (£8.50), lamb sausages with roast vegetables and balsamic vinegar (£8.75), and a very good home-made burger (£8.95); service is briskly efficient, and you may be greeted and shown to a table at busy times. Their half-dozen draught beers are mostly lagers, but also include Boddingtons; they have a good choice of wines, with half a dozen or so by the glass. The terrace may be heated in winter. Tate Modern and the rest of the South Bank attractions are a short stroll away. *Bar food (all day) ~ (020) 7928 6243 ~ Children welcome ~ Open 12(12.30 wknds)-11*

189. BARROW BOY & BANKER
Borough High St; ⊖/≋ London Bridge
Large elegant banking hall conversion with upper gallery, full Fullers
beer range kept well, decent wines, good manageress and efficient
young staff; popular food

190. BUNCH OF GRAPES
St Thomas St; ⊖/≋ London Bridge
Pleasant atmosphere, food counter in same good (french) hands
since the 1970s, well kept Youngs

191. HOLE IN THE WALL
Mepham St; ⊖/≋ Waterloo
Well kept changing ales such as Adnams, Everards Tiger, Youngs
Bitter and Special and their own Battersea Power Station, plenty of
lagers, and good malts and irish whiskeys, in welcoming no-frills
drinkers' dive in railway arch virtually underneath Waterloo –
rumbles and shakes with the trains; not a place for comfort-lovers, let
alone gastronomes; loudish jukebox, pinball and games machines
basic food such as sandwiches, ploughman's and salads all day (cl
wknd afternoons)

192. HORNIMAN
Hays Galleria, off Battlebridge Lane; ⊖/≋ London Bridge
Good stop on Thames walks, spacious, bright and airy, with lots of
polished wood, comfortable seating inc a few sofas, and a no
smoking area; Adnams, Bass, Fullers London Pride and Greene King
IPA, choice of teas and coffees at good prices, lunchtime bar food
from soup and big sandwiches to simple hot dishes, snacks at other
times; unobtrusive piped music; fine Thames views from picnic-sets
outside; open all day

193. LORD CLYDE
Clennam St; ⊖ Borough
Striking tilework outside; unpretentious panelled L-shaped main bar, small hatch-service back public bar with darts, real ales inc Fullers London Pride, Shepherd Neame Spitfire and Youngs; good value straightforward home-made food wkdy lunchtimes and early evenings, may do toasties, etc on request at other times (worth asking); welcoming service

194. MULBERRY BUSH
Upper Ground; ⊖/⇌ Waterloo
Attractively modernised, sympathetically lit Youngs pub, very handy for South Bank complex; open-plan with lots of wood, slightly raised turkey-carpeted balustraded area and small tiled-floor no smoking back conservatory; decent wines, helpful staff, well priced bar food; spiral stairs to bistro

195. PINEAPPLE
Hercules Rd; ⊖ Lambeth North
Friendly flower-decked pub with low-priced honest food from toasties and baked potatoes up, Bass, Fullers London Pride and Youngs; interesting maps of the area in the late 18th c, games room on right; picnic-sets out in front

196. WELLINGTON
Waterloo Rd; ⊖/⇌ Waterloo
Comfortably refurbished late-Victorian pub with large high-ceilinged linked rooms, light wood panelling, enormous stirring Battle of Waterloo murals on wall and ceiling; Adnams, Brakspears, Courage Directors, Youngs and a beer labelled for the pub from ornate bar counter, food all day, plenty of comfortable chairs and sofas, attractive tables, friendly service; can get very crowded despite its

size, sports TV; has had deaf people's night every other Fri; bedrooms; open all day

197. WHEATSHEAF
Stoney St; ⊖/⇌ London Bridge
Simple bare-boards Borough Market local, Youngs and a guest ale from central servery, decent wine choice, lunchtime food, friendly staff, some brown panelling; sports TV in one bar, piped music, games machine; tables on small back terrace and on pavement by market; open all day, cl Sun

SE3 (Blackheath)

198. HARE & BILLET
Eliot Cottages, Hare & Billet Rd; ⇌ Blackheath
Nicely matured, open-plan refurbishment of pub dating from 16th c, panelling, bare boards, good solid furniture and open fire, raised middle section; good value food, real ales such as Adnams, Bass, Fullers London Pride and Wadworths 6X; view over Blackheath

SE10 (Greenwich)

199. CUTTY SARK
Ballast Quay, off Lassell Street, SE10; ⇌ Maze Hill, from London Bridge; or, from the river front, walk past the Yacht in Crane Street and Trinity Hospital
It's hard not to imagine smugglers and blackguards with patches over their eyes at every turn in this attractive late 16th-c white-painted house. There are great views of the

Thames (and the Millennium Dome) both from the busy terrace across the narrow cobbled lane or, better still, from the upstairs room with the big bow window (itself striking for the way it jetties over the pavement). The bar has an old-fashioned feel, with flagstones, rough brick walls, wooden settles, barrel tables, open fires, low lighting and narrow openings to tiny side snugs; there's an elaborate central staircase. Changing beers such as Fullers London Pride, Greene King Abbot and Black Sheep on handpump, with a good choice of malt whiskies, and a decent wine list; fruit machine, jukebox. Served in a roomy eating area (and available all day during the week), bar food includes sandwiches, and changing hot dishes such as steak and ale pie, fish and chips or liver and bacon (around £6.25); Sunday roasts (£7.50). Service can slow down at busy times, and the pub can be alive with young people on Friday and Saturday evenings. They have jazz festivals two or three times a year, and Morris dancers occasionally drop by.
Bar food (12-9(6 wknds)) ~ Restaurant ~ (020) 8858 3146 ~ Children upstairs ~ Dogs allowed in bar ~ Open 11-11; 12-10.30 Sun

200. ADMIRAL HARDY
College Approach; Cutty Sark DLR
Large, recently redesigned open-plan pub retaining some nice portraits and stained glass; changing real ales such as Greene King Old Speckled Hen, Shepherd Neame Spitfire and Vale Black Swan Mild; reopened kitchen doing generous well prepared lunchtime

food, attached delicatessen; piped music; backs on to Greenwich Market

201. COACH & HORSES
Greenwich Market, Blackheath Rd; Cutty Sark DLR
Up-to-date food and young helpful staff; heated tables out in covered market

202. RICHARD I
Royal Hill; Greenwich DLR
Quietly old-fashioned pubby atmosphere, in friendly no-nonsense traditional two-bar local, with well kept Youngs; good staff, no piped music, bare boards, panelling; tables in pleasant back garden with barbecues; busy summer wknds and evenings

203. TRAFALGAR
Park Row; ≳ Maze Hill
Attractive and substantial 18th-c building with four elegant rooms inc pleasant dining room and central bar with lovely river-view bow window, careful colour schemes, oak panelling; helpful young staff welcoming even when busy (can get packed Fri and Sat evenings, may have bouncer then), good atmosphere; well prepared usual food inc speciality whitebait and good fresh veg, real ales inc Theakstons, good house wines; piped music in river-view room; handy for Maritime Museum, may have jazz wknds

204. YACHT
Crane St; ≳ Maze Hill
Friendly, neatly kept and civilised, with enjoyable food inc particularly good fish and chips, Adnams, Fullers London Pride, Greene King and Charles Wells Bombardier; good river view (Dome

too) from spacious room up a few steps from bar; cosy banquettes, light wood panelling, portholes, yacht pictures

SE11 (Kennington)

205. DOGHOUSE
Kennington Cross; ⊖ Kennington
Large and bright, with reasonably priced food, quieter side bar for locals and diners; may be loud music

206. PRINCE OF WALES
Cleaver Sq; ⊖ Kennington
Nicely placed traditional pub in quiet Georgian square, with well kept Shepherd Neame ales, pictures of notorious Londoners

207. SOUTH LONDON PACIFIC
Kennington Rd; ⊖ Oval
Former Cock Tavern converted to polynesian-theme bar, open 6pm till late; live music; cl Mon and some Suns

SE13 (Lewisham)

208. WATCH HOUSE
Lewisham High St; Lewisham DLR
Usual Wetherspoons style, good value special offers, well kept real ales inc three unusual changing guest beers; disabled facilities

SE16 (Docklands)

209. ANGEL
Bermondsey Wall East; ⊖ Bermondsey
Superb Thames views to Tower Bridge and the City upstream, and the Pool of London downstream, especially from balcony supported above water by great timber piles, and from picnic-sets in garden alongside; softly lit simply modernised bar with low-backed settles and old local photographs and memorablilia, food from baguettes to impressive main meals and good Sun roast, well kept cheap Sam Smiths, kind friendly staff; formal upstairs restaurant with waiter service; near remains of Edward III's palace, interesting walks round Surrey Quays

210. MAYFLOWER
Rotherhithe St; ⊖ Rotherhithe
Friendly and cosy old riverside pub with thriving local atmosphere despite growing emphasis on enjoyable food (not Sun night) from ciabatta rolls up; black beams, high-backed settles and coal fires, good views from calm upstairs restaurant (cl Sat lunchtime), well kept Greene King IPA and Abbot and a guest such as Black Sheep, good coffee and good value wines, quick friendly service; unobtrusive nostalgic piped music; children welcome, tables out on nice jetty/terrace over water; open all day; in unusual street with lovely Wren church

211. SHIP & WHALE
Gulliver St; ⊖ Surrey Quays
Small, neatly kept, opened-up pub with pleasant bar-style décor, full Shepherd Neame range kept well, welcoming young staff; enjoyable well presented fresh food from sandwiches up, choice of teas and

coffees, lots of board games; dogs welcome, small garden behind with barbecue

SE17 (Camberwell)

212. BEEHIVE
Carter St; ⊖ Kennington
Unpretentious bare-boards pub/bistro with well kept Courage Best and Directors and Fullers London Pride from island bar, cushioned pews, bric-a-brac on delft shelf, modern art in candlelit dining room; good choice of home-made food all day from sandwiches to steaks, wide range of wines, friendly service from neat staff; piped music, two TVs; tables outside

SE20 (Penge)

213. DR W G GRACE
Witham Rd; ⇌ Birkbeck
Themed after the cricketing pioneer, with lots of cricketing memorabilia; food all day, Courage Best and Directors, quiz nights Tues and Thurs, Sat party night, Sun prize box; children (till 7pm) and well behaved dogs welcome, family tables outside, adult roof terrace

SE21 (Dulwich)

214. CROWN & GREYHOUND
Dulwich Village, SE21; ⇌ North Dulwich

This big Edwardian pub has recently been extensively refurbished, and the main area, at the front, is now a roomy open bar, pleasantly furnished, with some quite ornate plasterwork and lamps over on the right, and a variety of nicely distinct seating areas from traditional upholstered and panelled settles to stripped kitchen tables on stripped boards, with a coal-effect gas fire and some Victorian prints. A big back dining room and conservatory opens into the pleasant garden, and there's an impressive welcome for families (with toys, changing facilities, and children's menus). Well kept Adnams, Fullers London Pride and Youngs on handpump (at pretty much central London prices); they have occasional beer festivals with up to 20 different brews. They do a good choice of well prepared home-made food. Changing every day, the lunchtime menu might include big doorstep sandwiches and ciabattas (from £2.95), soup (£3.80), and specials such as chicken in mustard sauce, lamb in red wine or cod mornay (all £6.95). Best to arrive early for their popular Sunday carvery (£8.70, or £7.20 for the vegetarian version), as they don't take bookings. Sandwiches are usually available all day, and there are barbecues at weekends. The family room is no smoking, as is the restaurant at lunchtime. The garden has lots of picnic-sets under a chestnut tree,

and a play area with sandpit. Known locally as the Dog, the pub was built at the turn of the 19th c to replace two inns that had stood here previously, hence the unusual name. Busy in the evenings, but quieter during the day, it's handy for walks through the park, and for the Dulwich Picture Gallery.
Bar food (12-10(9 Sun)) ~ Restaurant ~ (020) 8299 4976 ~ Children in no smoking area ~ Dogs allowed in bar ~ Open 11-11; 12-10.30 Sun

SE26 (Sydenham)

215. DULWICH WOOD HOUSE
Sydenham Hill; ≷ Sydenham Hill, but quite a walk
Well refurbished and extended Youngs pub in Victorian lodge gatehouse complete with turret; well kept ales, decent wines, attractively priced straightforward food cooked to order, popular at lunchtime with local retired people, friendly service; steps up to entrance; lots of tables in big pleasant back garden (no dogs) with old-fashioned street lamps and barbecues

SW4 (Clapham)

216. ABBEVILLE
Abbeville Rd; ⊖ Clapham Common
New dining pub with sturdy furnishings, rugs on dark boards, warm décor, fresh waitress-served food inc mediterranean specials and wknd brunches; Fullers ales and Timothy Taylors Landlord

217. ALEXANDRA
Clapham Common South Side; ⊖ Clapham Common

Good lively atmosphere (especially when football is screened), but always easy to get to the bar, with quick service from efficient friendly staff; good jukebox strong on indie/alternative music, some comedy nights and live music upstairs

218. COACH & HORSES
Clapham Park Rd; ⊖ Clapham Common

Traditionally refurbished and back to its original name; real ales and enjoyable food at reasonable prices, comfortable feel

219. WINDMILL
Clapham Common South Side; ⊖ Clapham Common

Big bustling well restored Victorian pub by the common, particularly worth knowing for its good well equipped bedrooms; civilised bar with sets of four deeply comfortable chairs around each table, plenty of pictures, coal fires and smaller areas opening off inc panelled back no smoking room; decent food (all day wknds) from soup and baguettes up, prompt friendly service, well kept Youngs Bitter, Special and seasonal beers, good choice of wines by the glass; piped music, TV; children in family room, dogs allowed in bar, open all day

SW8 (Lambeth/Battersea Park)

220. REBATOS
South Lambeth Road, SW8; ⊖ Vauxhall, but quite a walk (past five other tapas bars)

Where the MI6 secrets-packed laptop famously went missing in 2000, this friendly bar opened 20 years ago. We have known it from its earliest days – it's been gently smartened up since then, but without losing its welcoming relaxed feel, or the long row of bar stools by its nice zinc-topped bar counter, with a tempting range of tapas on show at one end. These include patatas bravas (delicious herbed and spiced roasties, £2.95), grilled sardines (£3), whitebait or boquerones (fried anchovies, £3.50), chorizo served hot (£3.75), kidneys in sherry or prawns in filo (£3.95), peppers (£4.25) and serrano ham freshly carved off a splendid haunch (£5.95). On the broad plychrome flooring tiles are modern chrome and wood tables with red plush button-back banquettes and stools, and the walls, with flickering candle-effect lamps, are a mass of cuttings, diplomas, bullfight posters and so forth; the elegant regency-style ceiling plasterwork and matching wall panels are something of a surprise. They have good sensibly priced spanish wines, and a fine array of spirits. Service is helpful and concerned, and the piped music is quite eclectic (salsa and jazz, not just spanish). There is a sizeable back restaurant; the lavatories are upstairs.

Bar food (12-3; 5.30-10.45; 7-10.45 Sat; not Sun) ~
Restaurant ~ (020) 7735 6388 ~ Children welcome ~ Open 12-3, 5.30-10.45; 7-10.45 Sat; cl Sat lunchtime, Sun, bank hols, and around 10 days over Christmas and New Year

221. CANTON ARMS
South Lambeth Rd; ⊖ Vauxhall, but quite a walk
Recently refurbished, now has good welcoming atmosphere and enjoyable generous proper pub food

222. MASONS ARMS
Battersea Park Rd; ⇄ Battersea Park
Enjoyable generous bistro-style food, good value, changing local art for sale; lively evenings, especially wknds with DJs; tables out at the side

SW11 (Battersea)

223. FOX & HOUNDS
Latchmere Road, SW11; ⇄ Clapham Junction
The second of the small chain run by the two brothers who transformed the Atlas (*see* West London section), this big Victorian local has a similar emphasis on excellent mediterranean food. But what's particularly nice is that this still feels very much the kind of place where locals happily come to drink – and they're a more varied bunch than you might find filling the Atlas. The bright, spacious bar has bare boards, mismatched tables and chairs, two narrow pillars supporting the dark red ceiling, some attractive photographs on the walls, and big windows overlooking the street (the view partially obscured by colourful window boxes). There are fresh flowers and daily papers on the bar, and a view of the kitchen behind. Two rooms lead off, one rather cosy with its two red leatherette sofas. Changing every day,

the bar food might include lunchtime sandwiches, spinach soup with cream, nutmeg and croûtons (£3.50), linguine with pancetta, field mushrooms, rosemary, cream and parmesan (£6.50), pan-roast fillet of trout (£8), grilled marinated fillet of salmon with harissa, grilled aubergine and roast tomato salad, and cucumber and yoghurt salsa (£9.50), pan-roast pigeon breasts with grilled polenta, red onions, and rocket and parmesan salad (£10), grilled rib-eye steak with sautéed potatoes, green beans, and salsa verde (£11.50), creamy italian cheese with grilled bread and pear (£5), and chocolate and almond cake (£4). The pub can fill quickly, so you may have to move fast to grab a table. Well kept Bass, Fullers London Pride and a guest like Shepherd Neame Spitfire on handpump; the carefully chosen wine list (which includes around ten by the glass) is written out on a blackboard. The appealingly varied piped music fits in rather well. There are several tables in a garden behind. The same team have opened a further two similarly organised pubs: the Cumberland Arms near Olympia, and the Swan in Chiswick. *Bar food (12-2.30(3 Sat and Sun), 7-10; not Mon lunchtime) ~ (020) 7924 5483 ~ Children welcome till 7pm ~ Dogs allowed in bar ~ Open 12-3, 5-11; 12-11(10.30 Sun) Sat; cl Mon lunchtime; 24 Dec-1 Jan; Easter Sat and Sun*

224. CASTLE
Battersea High St; ⇌ Clapham Junction, long walk
Cosy atmosphere, enjoyable changing food, good short wine list; pretty garden

SW12 (Balham)

225. BEDFORD
Bedford Hill; ⊖/≷ Balham

Former hotel converted into pub, good use of all that space; enjoyable food, lively young bustle, sports TV; busy Fri and Sat with late night licence upstairs, live music, comedy, even dance classes

226. DUKE OF DEVONSHIRE
Balham High Rd; ⊖/≷ Balham

Old-fashioned large Victorian pub with original fittings, enjoyable food; tables outside front and back, open till 1am Fri and Sat

227. EXHIBIT
Balham Station Rd; ⊖/≷ Balham

Good atmosphere in bar with fine aquarium, enjoyable food, restaurant upstairs

SW13 (Barnes)

228. BRIDGE
Castelnau Gardens, SW13; ⊖ Hammersmith, but some distance away

It's well worth the walk over Hammersmith Bridge away from the clutch of pubs beside the river; the views from this superior gastro-pub may not be as good, but the food is far more interesting than at any of its better-placed rivals. The highlight of the spacious well refurbished bar is the comfortable, very separate-seeming area in the middle, with sofas and large wooden tables arranged around a big fireplace, underneath an unexpected chandelier. The area at the front is more traditional, with polished wooden floors, rich red walls, fresh flowers, and several intimate high-backed booths with leatherette cushions. The open-plan kitchen is behind the bar counter. A no smoking dining room at the back looks out over a particularly well landscaped garden, with tables on decking among fairy-lit trees and tropical plants. Served throughout the pub, the seasonally changing menu might include a substantial clam chowder (£5.50), good sausages with mash, parsnips and caramelised onion gravy (£7.50), huge home-made fish fingers (£7.95), tuna burger (£9.50), and a variety of more elaborate meals; they usually do a two-course menu for £12 between 5.30 and 6.30pm, and have a separate menu for weekend brunch and Sunday lunch. They have a particularly good range of wines, with up to a dozen by the glass, and some unusual champagnes; well kept Greene King Ruddles County, Marstons Pedigree and Charles Wells Bombardier on handpump. Piped music, fruit machine.

Bar food (all day) ~ Restaurant (12-3, 5.30-10.30, supper licence till 12) ~ (020) 8563 9811 ~ Children in restaurant ~ Open 12-11

229. BULLS HEAD
Lonsdale Road, SW13; ⇄ Barnes Bridge

Top-class live jazz is this busy Thames-side pub's main claim to fame. Every night for the last 40 years internationally renowned jazz and blues groups have performed here; you can hear the music quite clearly from the lounge bar (and on peaceful Sunday afternoons from the villagey little street as you approach), but for the full effect and genuine jazz-club atmosphere it is worth paying the admission to the well equipped music room. Bands play 8.30-11 every night plus 2-4.30pm Sundays, and depending on who's playing prices generally range from £4 to around £10. The big, simply furnished and decorated bar has photographs of many of the musicians who've played here, as well as a couple of cosier areas leading off, and an island servery with Youngs Bitter, Special and seasonal beers on handpump. They keep over 70 malt whiskies, and have a particularly impressive wine list, running to 240 bottles at the last count, with around 30 by the glass. A short range of good value bar food (all home-made, with nothing frozen) includes soup (£2), sandwiches (from £3), a hot dish of the day (£4.90), and a daily roast (£5.50); there's usually something available all day, and in the evening they do good thai food in the Stables restaurant. Service is efficient and friendly. Dominoes, cribbage, Scrabble, chess, cards, TV. One room is no smoking.
Bar food (12-11) ~ Restaurant ~ (020) 8876 5241 ~
Children in family room ~ Dogs allowed in bar ~ Jazz and

blues every night and Sun lunchtime ~ Open 11-11;
12-10.30 Sun

230. IDLE HOUR
**Railway Side (off White Hart Lane between Mortlake High St
and Upper Richmond Rd); ⇌ Barnes Bridge**
Out of the way small local transformed into friendly organic gastro-
pub, very good individually cooked food inc choice of Sun roasts,
splendid bloody mary, good range of organic soft drinks, Flowers
IPA; nice chunky old tables on bare boards, relaxed atmosphere,
daily papers and magazines, a profusion of wall clocks, comfortable
sofa by small fireplace; chill-out piped music, cl wkdy lunchtimes, no
children; tables with candles and cocktail parasols out in small pretty
yard behind, elaborate barbecues; if driving, park at end of Railway
Side and walk – the road quickly becomes too narrow for cars

231. SUN
Church Rd; ⇌ Barnes Bridge
Attractive spot with tables overlooking duckpond; recently done up
inside, with sofas, tuscan wall colours and tracked spotlights; several
areas around central servery, real ales, home-cooked food with
italian leanings from good paninis up, prompt service even though
busy; prices on the high side, piped music may be loud

SW14 (Sheen)

232. VICTORIA
West Temple Sheen, SW14; ⇌ Mortlake
A short stroll from Richmond Park's Sheen Gate, this once-
incongruous local has been radically reworked over the last

few years, and is now a stylish gastro-pub with rooms, very well regarded for its superior food and as a peaceful place to stay. The management's pedigree in some of London's most famous kitchens quickly becomes obvious, but that doesn't make it at all stuffy or self-important – in fact quite the opposite: though firmly upmarket, it still has the air of a favourite neighbourhood drop-in eating place. At lunchtimes it's popular with families, when children can enjoy the sheltered play area in the back garden while parents supervise from the conservatory, but it's in the evenings that we've enjoyed it most; it's particularly civilised and sophisticated then, and the huge glass room at the back seems especially stunning. Leading into that is essentially one big thoughtfully designed room, with wooden floors and armchairs, and separate-seeming areas with a fireplace, sofas, and plenty of contemporary touches. They open at 8.30 for breakfast and after that the kitchen doesn't really close, serving morning coffee, lunch, tea and cake, and finally dinner. The menu changes every day, but might include things like piquillo peppers stuffed with smoked haddock brandade and salsa verde (£6.95), serrano ham with celeriac remoulade and truffle oil (£7.95), penne with roast walnut sauce, wilted rocket and pecorino (£9.95), braised wild rabbit with red wine, bacon and mushrooms (£11.95), and grilled bass with basil mash, bouillabaisse sauce and rouille (£15.95). Their tapas plate is a popular starter (£8.95), and they have a weekend brunch menu with dishes such as pumpkin gnocchi with parmesan cream and crisp sage (£4.95 small, £6.95 large), wild boar and apple sausages with mash and onion gravy (£5.95 small, £7.95 large), and duck confit hash with a fried egg, bacon and their own herb ketchup (£7.95). The wine list is very good, and they have various unusual sherries and malts; also Brakspears (not cheap). Bedrooms (in a secluded annexe) are simple but smart.

Bar food (all day) ~ Restaurant (12-2.30(3 wknds), 7-10(9 Sun)) ~ (020) 8876 4238 ~ Children welcome ~ Open 8.30-12; 11-12 Sat; 11-11.30 Sun ~ Bedrooms: £82.50B/£92.50B

SW15 (Putney)

233. DUKES HEAD
Lower Richmond Rd; ⊖ Putney Bridge, and cross river
Classic Victorian Youngs pub, spacious and grand yet friendly, light and airy with big ceiling fans, very civilised feel, tables by window with great Thames view; well kept ales, 20 wines by the glass, good value fresh lunchtime food, coal fires; smaller more basic locals' bar, plastic glasses for outside

234. HALF MOON
Lower Richmond Rd; ⇌ Mortlake
Genuine pub with nice atmosphere, well kept Youngs, enjoyable food, good friendly service; popular live music nights

235. JOLLY GARDENERS
Lacy Rd; ⇌ Putney
Stylishly redecorated cool bar with draught belgian beers, good wine list, interesting choice of enjoyable food, lots of sofas, trendy artwork, chill-out music; nice tables on tiny back terrace

236. OLDE SPOTTED HORSE
Putney High St; ⇌ Putney
Large recently refurbished open-plan bar with island servery, good range of food at reasonable prices from on-view kitchen, well kept Youngs, good wine choice, quick efficient service

237. PUTNEY PAGE
Lower Richmond Rd; ⇌ Barnes
Spacious and brightly refurbished local near Putney Common (formerly the Spencer Arms); open-plan with pale wooden floor and fittings, cushioned seats under curved windows, matt black marble dining tables, lots of spotlights, some rowing memorabilia inc big picture of first Boat Race in 1829; Fullers London Pride and Charles Wells Bombardier, friendly, chatty service; kitchen specialises in enjoyable thai/japanese food, also burgers; piped music, muted plasma screen TVs for sport, occasional live music and events

SW17 (Wandsworth Common)

238. HOPE
Bellevue Rd; ⇌ Wandsworth Common
After a spell as a Firkin, now back to its proper name, heading upmarket with appealing food and Wandsworth Common views

SW18 (Wandsworth)

239. ALMA
York Road, SW18; ⇌ Wandsworth Town

Feeling lighter and airier since a slight refurbishment, this relaxed and comfortable corner pub is very much like a welcoming local, but a rather smart one – and the distinctive food lifts it well out of the ordinary. The furnishings are mostly quite simple: a mix of chairs and cast-iron-framed or worn wooden tables around the brightly repainted walls, and a couple of sofas, with gilded mosaics of the 19th-c Battle of the Alma and an ornate mahogany chimney-piece and fireplace adding a touch of elegance. The popular but less pubby dining room has a fine turn-of-the-19th-c frieze of swirly nymphs, and a new window overlooking an ornamental garden; there's waitress service in here, and you can book a particular table. Youngs Bitter, Special and seasonal brews from the island bar counter, and good house wines (with around 20 by the glass), freshly squeezed juices, good coffee, tea or hot chocolate; newspapers out for customers. Even when it's very full – which it often is in the evenings – service is careful and efficient. The imaginative and generously served bar food might include very good sandwiches (from £3.75), soups such as roasted fennel and parsnip (£3.75), falafels with warm potato, chargrilled courgette and spring onion and cucumber salad (£7.95), spaghetti with english asparagus, salmon and lemon cream

(£8.50), and seared lamb with ginger lentils and bok choi (£9.50); the menu is a little different on Sundays, when they do various roasts. Much of the meat is organic, and comes from their own farm in Dorking. If you're after a quiet drink don't come when there's a rugby match on the television, unless you want a running commentary from the well heeled and spoken young locals. Pinball, dominoes. Charge up their 'smart-card' with cash and you can pay with a discount either here or at the management's other pubs, which include the Ship in Wandsworth (see below). Travelling by rail into Waterloo you can see the pub rising above the neighbouring rooftops as you rattle through Wandsworth Town.
Bar food (12-4, 6-10; 12-4 Sun) ~ Restaurant ~ (020) 8870 2537 ~ Children welcome ~ Open 11-11; 12-10.30 Sun; cl 25 Dec

240. SHIP

Jews Row, SW18; ⇌ Wandsworth Town

Always packed on sunny days, this relaxed riverside pub has an excellent barbecue every day in summer, and at winter weekends. Serving very good home-made burgers and sausages, marinated lamb steaks, goats cheese quesidillas, and even cajun chicken and lobster; it's all-weather, with plenty of covered areas if necessary. The extensive terrace has lots of picnic-sets, pretty hanging baskets and brightly coloured flowerbeds, small trees, and an outside bar; a Thames barge is moored alongside. They do a particularly appealing menu inside too, as at the Alma above (under the same management), relying very much on free-range produce, much of it from Mr Gotto's farm; a typical choice might include poached pear, prosciutto and taleggio cheese (£4.45), spring onion pancake with home-cured gravadlax (£4.95), lemon and garlic corn-fed chicken with chilli rice and wilted spinach (£8.95), fried darne of salmon with chinese leaves, creamed potatoes and parsley and pesto sauce (£8.90), fillet of pork with potato gratin, green beans and stilton sauce (£9.50), and barbary duck breast with fresh mango and cassis gravy (£11.50). You can book tables (except at Sunday lunchtimes), and there's something available all day. Only a small part of the original ceiling is left in the main bar – the rest is in a light and airy conservatory style, with wooden tables, a medley of stools, and old church chairs on the floorboards. One part has a Victorian fireplace, a huge clock surrounded by barge prints, an old-fashioned bagatelle board, and jugs of flowers around the window sills. The basic public bar has plain wooden furniture, a black kitchen range in the fireplace, and a jukebox. The atmosphere is laid-back and chatty, and it's a great favourite with smart local twenty-somethings. Well kept Youngs Bitter, Special and seasonal brews on handpump, with freshly squeezed orange and other fruit juices, a wide range of wines (a dozen or more by the glass), and a good choice of teas and coffees. Helpful service from pleasant staff. Alas, their famous fireworks display is no more (not the pub's

fault), but they still have a rousing celebration on the last
night of the Proms. The adjacent car park can fill pretty quickly.
Bar food (12-11(10.30 Sun)) ~ Restaurant ~
(020) 8870 9667 ~ Children welcome ~ Dogs allowed in
bar ~ Open 11-11; 12-10.30 Sun

241. OLD SERGEANT
Garratt Lane; ≥ Wandsworth Town
Classic, homely and unspoilt two-bar local with long-serving
landlord; Youngs full range kept well, wkdy lunches, friendly efficient
service, good Christmas decorations; open all day

SW19 (Wimbledon)

242. CROOKED BILLET
Wimbledon Common; ⊖/≥ Wimbledon quite a walk
Popular olde-worlde pub by common, lovely spot in summer, open
all day; full Youngs range kept well, well cooked generous food,
pleasant helpful service; lots of old prints, nice furnishings on broad
polished oak boards, soft lighting, daily papers; restaurant in 16th-c
barn behind

243. SULTAN
Norman Rd; ⊖ South Wimbledon
Proper drinking pub emphasising well kept Hop Back ales such as
Summer Lightning and Crop Circle; sandwiches and toasties, darts in
public bar with trophies in corner, big scrubbed tables inside and
out; good courtyard

Richmond

244. WHITE CROSS
Water Lane, Richmond; ⊖/⇌ Richmond

The setting of this Thames-side pub is perfect – it's a delightful spot in summer, and has a certain wistful charm in winter as well. On fine days, when it can get rather crowded, the busy paved garden in front can feel a little like a cosmopolitan seaside resort; plenty of tables overlook the water, and in summer there's an outside bar. Inside, the two chatty main rooms have something of the air of the hotel this once was, with local prints and photographs, an old-fashioned wooden island servery, and a good mix of variously aged customers. Two of the three log fires have mirrors above them – unusually, the third is below a window. A bright and airy upstairs room has lots more tables, and a pretty cast-iron balcony opening off, with a splendid view down to the river, and a couple more tables and chairs. Well kept Youngs Bitter, Special and seasonal beers on handpump, and a good range of 15 or so carefully chosen wines by the glass; service is friendly and civilised, even when the pub is at its busiest. Fruit machine, dominoes. From a servery at the foot of the stairs, lunchtime bar food includes good sandwiches (from £2.60), salads (from £5.75), a variety of sausages (£6.50), and good daily-changing home-made dishes such as pasta (£6.25), mixed game pie (£6.75), and a daily roast. Take care if you're leaving your car along the river near this popular Thames-side pub, it pays to check the tide times; one customer discovered just how fast the water can rise when on returning to his vehicle he found it marooned in a rapidly swelling pool of water, and had to paddle out shoeless to retrieve it. It's not unknown for the water to reach right up the steps into the bar, completely covering anything that gets in the way. Boats leave from immediately outside for Kingston and Hampton Court.

Bar food (12-4) ~ (020) 8940 6844 ~ Dogs welcome ~
Open 11-11; 12-10.30 Sun

WEST LONDON

SW5 (Earls Court)

245. BLACKBIRD
Earls Court Rd; ⊖ Earls Court

Big comfortable bank conversion, dark panelling, plenty of nooks and corners; decent lunchtime food especially home-made pies and freshly carved roasts in barm cakes, full range of Fullers ales kept well; interesting pictures; open all day

246. KINGS HEAD
Hogarth Pl/Fenway St; ⊖ Earls Court

Bass and Fullers London Pride and food such as sandwiches, caesar salad, risotto and aberdeen angus burger, in corner pub with horseshoe bar and dining chairs and tables on bare boards

SW6 (Fulham)

247. ATLAS
Seagrave Road, SW6; ⊖ West Brompton

The first of a burgeoning little chain set up by two brothers, this is a particularly rewarding food pub, with imaginative, reasonably priced meals, an excellent, carefully chosen wine list, and a good, buzzy atmosphere. If there's a downside it's simply the place's popularity – tables are highly prized, so if you're planning to eat, arrive early, or swoop quickly. Listed on a blackboard above the brick fireplace, and changing every day, the sensibly short choice of food might include pea, parsnip and mint soup with parmesan crostini (£3.50), very good antipasti (£6), smoked duck breast salad with green beans, roasted tomatoes and rocket (£7.50), delicious grilled tuscan sausages with borlotti beans, garlic, rosemary, parsley and roast red onions (£8), pot-roast half chicken with lemon and thyme, fennel roast potatoes and tomato chilli jam, or moroccan beef casserole with paprika, cinnamon, vanilla and cayenne (£10.50), and pan-roast sea bass with vine tomatoes, basil, black olives and capers (£11.50); they may have a good cake like lemon and rosemary with whiskey cream (£4), or soft italian cheese with apple and grilled bread (£5). With a pleasantly bustling feel in the evenings (it's perhaps not the place for a cosy quiet dinner), the long, simple knocked-together bar has been well renovated without removing the original features; there's plenty of panelling and dark wooden wall benches, with a mix of school chairs and well spaced tables. Smart young people figure prominently in the mix, but there are plenty of locals too, as well as visitors to the Exhibition Centre at Earls Court (one of the biggest car parks is next door). Well kept Charles Wells Bombardier, Fullers London Pride, and a guest like Brakspears or Greene King IPA on handpump, and a changing selection of around ten wines by the glass; big mugs of coffee. Friendly service. The piped music is unusual – on various visits we've come across everything from salsa and jazz to vintage TV themes; it can be loud at times. Down at the end is a TV, by a hatch to the kitchen. Outside is an

attractively planted narrow side terrace, with an overhead awning; heaters make it comfortable even in winter. Another of their pubs, the Fox & Hounds, is a main entry in the South London section.
Bar food (12.30-3, 7-(10 Sun)10.30) ~ (020) 7385 9129 ~
Children welcome till 7pm ~ Dogs welcome ~
Open 12-11(10.30 Sun); cl 23 Dec-2 Jan

248. WHITE HORSE
Parsons Green, SW6; ⊖ Parsons Green

Though it's well liked for its food and efficient service, this splendidly organised pub is perhaps best known for its impressively eclectic range of drinks. Six perfectly kept real ales include Adnams Broadside, Bass, Harveys Sussex, Highgate Mild, Oakham JHB, Roosters Yankee, and rapidly changing guests; they also keep 15 Trappist beers, around 50 other foreign bottled beers, a dozen malt whiskies, and a constantly expanding range of good, interesting and reasonably priced wines. Every item on the menu, whether it be scrambled egg or raspberry and coconut tart, has a suggested accompaniment listed beside it, perhaps a wine, perhaps a bottled beer. They're keen to encourage people to select beer with food as you might wine, and organise regular beer dinners where every course comes with a recommended brew. Good bar food might include soup, sandwiches (from £4), ploughman's (with some unusual cheeses, £5), twice-baked cheese soufflé with caramelised onions (£6.25), warm chorizo salad (£6.75), salmon fishcakes with tarragon mayonnaise, or pork sausages and mash (£7.75), beer-battered cod and chips (£8.25), fennel risotto with parmesan and truffle oil (£8.50), fried bass with garlic mash, capers, mint and brown butter (£12.75), and daily specials. There's usually something to eat available all day; at weekends they do a good brunch menu, and in winter they do a popular Sunday lunch. The stylishly modernised U-shaped bar has plenty of sofas, wooden tables, and huge windows with slatted wooden blinds, and winter coal and log fires, one in an elegant marble fireplace. The pub is usually busy (and can feel crowded at times), but there are enough smiling, helpful staff behind the solid panelled central servery to ensure you'll rarely have to wait too long to be served. All the art displayed is for sale. The back restaurant is no smoking. On summer evenings the front terrace overlooking the green has something of a continental feel, with crowds of people drinking al fresco; there may be Sunday barbecues. They have quarterly beer festivals (often spotlighting regional breweries), as well as lively celebrations on American Independence Day or Thanksgiving.

Bar food (12(11 Sat and Sun)-10.30) ~ Restaurant ~
(020) 7736 2115 ~ Children welcome ~ Dogs allowed in bar ~ Open 11-11; 12-10.30 Sun; cl 25-26 Dec

249. DUKE OF CUMBERLAND
New Kings Rd; ⊖ Parsons Green

Huge lavishly restored Edwardian pub, attractive decorative tiles and interesting panel fleshing out the Duke's life; sofas, coffee tables and candles; well kept Youngs Bitter and Special, cheerful at wknd lunchtimes, relaxed for wkdy lunchtime food (no food Fri-Sun evenings); big-screen sports TV in sanded-floor main bar (smaller carpeted back area), piped pop music may be loud, can get smoky in evenings; open all day; a few tables out in side street

SW7 (South Kensington)

250. ANGLESEA ARMS
Selwood Terrace, SW7; ⊖ South Kensington

Managing to feel both smart and cosy at the same time, this genuinely old-fashioned pub is currently well-regarded for its food, as well as its particularly friendly, chatty atmosphere. In summer the place to be is the leafy front patio (with outside heaters for chillier evenings), but it's really rather nice in winter, when the elegant and individual bar seems especially enticing. On busy days you'll need to move fast to grab a seat, but most people seem happy leaning on the central elbow tables. There's a mix of cast-iron tables on the bare wood-strip floor, panelling, and big windows with attractive swagged curtains; at one end several booths with partly glazed screens have cushioned pews and spindleback chairs. The traditional mood is heightened by some heavy portraits, prints of London and large brass chandeliers. A good choice of real ales takes in Adnams Bitter and Broadside, Brakspears, Fullers London Pride, Youngs Special and a weekly changing guest like Greene King Abbot; also a few bottled belgian beers, around 20 whiskies, and a varied wine list, with everything available by the glass. Downstairs is a separate eating area, with a Victorian fireplace. The lunchtime menu typically includes sandwiches and paninis (from £5.55), soup (£3.50), welsh rarebit with crispy bacon topping (£4.25), scallops wrapped in smoked bacon with a warm sage and olive dressing (£6.95), steak and kidney pie (£6.95), cumberland sausage and mash with beer and onion gravy (£7.25), home-made fishcakes (£7.55), and stuffed peppers with couscous and ratatouille with melted goats cheese (£7.95); in the evening they add things like mussels in a provençale or white wine and cream sauce (£8.25) and venison on a bed of rösti and spinach with veal jus (£12.95). Good all-day Sunday roasts. Service is friendly and helpful. *Bar food (12-3, 6.30-10; 12-10 Sat and Sun) ~ Restaurant ~ (020) 7373 7960 ~ Children in eating area of bar and restaurant ~ Dogs allowed in bar ~ Open 11-11; 12-10.30 Sun*

SW10 (Chelsea/Fulham)

251. WATER RAT
Kings Rd; ⊖ Fulham Broadway
Small pub specialising in reasonably priced, tasty lebanese food;
Adnams and Youngs, arty nude photographs, civilised atmosphere
(but for SkyTV football and chain-smoking Chelsea fans on match
days)

W3 (Acton)

252. CHURCHFIELD
Churchfield Rd; ⇌ Acton Central
Nicely reworked former station building; quite a grand upstairs
dining room with attractively priced good food and good wine
choice, proper bar with wide range of beers, helpful friendly staff;
tables outside

W4 (Chiswick)

253. BULLS HEAD
Strand on the Green, W4; ⊖/⇌ Kew
Now a Chef & Brewer, this nicely refurbished riverside pub
has a greater emphasis on food than it did in the past, but
remains an atmospheric place for a cosy drink, in a fine spot
by the narrow towpath. There's a comfortably traditional feel
to the series of pleasant little rooms rambling through black-
panelled alcoves and up and down steps; old-fashioned

benches are built into the simple panelling, and small windows look past attractively planted hanging flower baskets to the river. Lots of empty wine bottles are dotted around, and there's plenty of polished dark wood and beams. Served all day, the big menu takes in everything from filled baguettes (£4.99), through fish and chips (£5.95) and beef and ale pie (£6.95), to beef wellington (£15.95); Sunday roasts. Around half the pub is no smoking. Fullers London Pride, Greene King Old Speckled Hen, and Theakstons Best on handpump; newspapers are laid out for customers. The original building served as Cromwell's HQ several times during the Civil War, and it was here that Moll Cutpurse overheard Cromwell talking to Fairfax about the troops' pay money coming by horse from Hounslow, and got her gang to capture the moneybags; they were later recovered at Turnham Green.

Bar food (11-10; 12-9.30 Sun) ~ Restaurant ~
(020) 8994 1204 ~ Children in eating area of bar ~
Open 11-11; 12-10.30 Sun

254. BELL & CROWN
Strand on the Green; ⊖/≩ Kew

Big busy Fullers local with their standard beers kept well, several comfortable areas, local paintings and photographs; good value food inc interesting dishes, efficient friendly staff, log fire, no piped music or machines; great Thames views especially from conservatory and picnic-sets out by towpath (good walks); open all day

255. BOLLO HOUSE
Bollo Lane; ⊖ Chiswick Park
Spacious modern bar/bistro with sofas, light-coloured furniture and amber walls above pale dado; up-to-date food, Greene King IPA and Abbot, daily papers; tables outside

256. CITY BARGE
Strand on the Green; ⊖/⇌ Kew
Small panelled riverside bars, not over-modernised and with nice original features, in picturesque partly 15th-c pub (the original part reserved for diners lunchtime); also airy newer back part done out with maritime signs and bird prints; sensibly priced bar food (not Sun) from sandwiches up, well kept Fullers London Pride and Charles Wells Bombardier, back conservatory, winter fires; some tables on towpath – lovely spot to watch sun set over Kew Bridge

W5 (Ealing)

257. WHEATSHEAF
Haven Lane; ⊖ Ealing Broadway
Big, pleasant, flower-decked Fullers pub with cheerful bare-boards bar, their full beer range, friendly service, sandwiches, salads and hot dishes at sensible prices; enormous log fire in back room

W6 (Hammersmith)

258. ANGLESEA ARMS
Wingate Road, W6; ⊖ Ravenscourt Park
One reader considers the food at this superior gastro-pub to be the best within a 50-mile radius, so though it's rather off

the beaten path, it is well worth tracking down. Changing every lunchtime and evening, the inventive menu might include starters such as asparagus and broad bean soup (£3.95), tomato, aubergine, onion and thyme tartlet (£4.95), breadcrumbed escalope of rabbit, with spinach, lemon, garlic and mustard fruits (£5.25), and moroccan stuffed squid with couscous, raisins and cumin (£5.50), half a dozen irish rock oysters with Guinness bread and shallot relish (£7.25), a short choice of main courses like stuffed globe artichoke, ceps, asparagus, soft duck egg, toasted brioche and rocket (£7.95), monkfish brochette with parma ham, grilled peppers, courgettes and basil (£8.25), pot-roast corn-fed chicken breast with garlic mash and baby vegetables (£8.50), or sautéed calves liver with pancetta, puy lentils, capers, sage and cabernet sauvignon (£9.75), and some unusual farmhouse cheeses (£4.95); they usually do a set menu at lunchtimes, with two courses for £9.95. The bustling eating area leads off the bar but feels quite separate, with skylights creating a brighter feel, closely packed tables, and a big modern painting along one wall; directly opposite is the kitchen, with several chefs frantically working on the meals. You can't book, so best to get there early for a table, or be prepared to wait. It feels a lot more restauranty than, say, the Eagle (p5), though you can also eat in the bar: rather plainly decorated, but cosy in winter when the roaring fire casts long flickering shadows on the dark panelling. Neatly stacked piles of wood guard either side of the fireplace (which has a stopped clock above it), and there are some well worn green leatherette chairs and stools. Courage Best, Fullers London Pride and guest like Adnams Broadside or Shepherd Neame Spitfire on handpump, with a wide range of carefully chosen wines listed above the bar. Several tables outside overlook the quiet street (not the easiest place to find a parking space). *Bar food (12.30–2.45(3 Sat, 3.30 Sun), 7.30-10.30(9.45 Sun)) ~ Restaurant ~ (020) 8749 1291 ~ Children welcome ~ Dogs allowed in bar ~ Open 11-11(10.30 Sun); cl Christmas for one week, 1 Jan*

259. BROOK GREEN
Shepherds Bush Road, W6; ⊖ Hammersmith

Once eminently avoidable, this big Victorian hotel is enjoying something of a renaissance under its enterprising current management. They've spruced up the décor, opened probably the area's most appealing bedrooms, and introduced a series of varied events in the downstairs wine bar, including regular comedy and blues nights with some well known acts. On our last visit they were staging an opera night, which meant there was perhaps an even greater variety of customers packed in than usual, from burly local builders to bow-tied culture buffs, plus everything in between. Rambling round a sizeable central bar counter, the single spacious room has lofty ceilings, some impressive plasterwork, comfortably cushioned banquettes under ornately framed mirrors, a big fireplace, and occasional gold circles and lines punctuating the red-painted walls. Big screens are used particularly for rugby; at other times they may be on with the sound turned down. Changing bar food might include things like vegetable and brie burritos with green salad (£6), a hefty home-made 12oz burger (£6.50), cod and gruyère cakes with tomato hollandaise (£7.50), and perhaps themed dishes to tie in with brewery promotions. At the back is a small terrace, with tables under umbrellas, and a fair amount of bamboo. There's a no smoking area to the right of the entrance; other areas can seem smoky at busy times. Well kept Youngs Bitter, Special and seasonal brews on handpump, and a good range of wines, with over two dozen by the glass; friendly service. They open from 7am for breakfasts. Nearby parking can be tricky.

Bar food (12-3, 6-10, though see above for breakfasts) ~ Restaurant ~ (020) 7602 1777 ~ Children welcome away from bar ~ Weekly blues (Thurs) and comedy (Fri) in downstairs bar, with late licence ~ Open 11-11; 12-10.30 Sun ~ Bedrooms: £79B/£89B

260. DOVE

Upper Mall, W6; ⊖ Ravenscourt Park

London has plenty of spots from which to admire its river, but the delightful back terrace of this old-fashioned Thames-side tavern is one of the nicest. The main flagstoned area, down some steps, has a few highly prized teak tables and white metal and teak chairs looking over the low river wall to the

Thames reach just above Hammersmith Bridge, and there's a tiny exclusive area up a spiral staircase. If you're able to bag a spot here, you'll often see rowing crews out on the water. By the entrance from the quiet alley, the front bar is cosy and traditional, with black panelling, and red leatherette cushioned built-in wall settles and stools around dimpled copper tables; it leads to a bigger, similarly furnished room, with old framed advertisements and photographs of the pub. They stock the full range of Fullers beers, with well kept Chiswick, ESB, London Pride and seasonal beers on handpump: no games machines or piped music. It's not quite so crowded at lunchtimes as it is in the evenings. Served all day (except Sunday), bar food might include sandwiches, fishcakes, lamb burgers in pitta bread (£5.95), steak and ESB pie (£7.25), and king prawns with garlic and rice (£7.95). A plaque marks the level of the highest-ever tide in 1928. Note: they don't allow children. The pub is said to be where *Rule Britannia* was composed.

Bar food (12-9(4 Sat)) ~ (020) 8748 5405 ~ Children welcome away from bar ~ Dogs welcome ~ Open 11-11; 12-10.30 Sun

261. BLACK LION
South Black Lion Lane; ⊖ Stamford Brook
Welcoming and civilised cottagey pub, helpful staff; Courage Best and Directors, decent usual food from baguettes and baked potatoes up, dining area behind big log-effect gas fire; large pleasant heated terrace

262. CRABTREE
Rainville Rd; ⊖ Barons Court quite a walk
Spacious and comfortable conversion, light and airy, with big
settees, bookcases, good choice of ciabattas and sandwiches, also
hot dishes, good range of wines by the glass; handy for Thames Path
and Bishops Park

263. THATCHED HOUSE
Dalling Rd; ⊖ Ravenscourt Park
Spacious Youngs dining pub with their full beer range and enjoyable
food (not Mon or Tues, or Sun eve) – though local drinkers still
come; stripped pine, modern art, big armchairs, good wine list, welcoming staff and regulars, conservatory; no music; open all day
wknds

W7 (Hanwell)

264. FOX
Green Lane; ⇌ Hanwell
Friendly, open-plan, 19th-c pub in quiet cul de sac near Grand
Union Canal; well kept real ales, decent wines, good value
wholesome food from good toasties, baguettes and baked potatoes
to home-made hot dishes inc Sun roasts; dining area, panelling and
stained glass one end, wildlife pictures and big fish tank, farm tools
hung from ceiling; smoking throughout; darts end, small side garden,
occasional wknd barbecues, towpath walks

W8 (Kensington)

265. CHURCHILL ARMS
Kensington Church Street, W8; ⊖ Notting Hill Gate or Kensington High Street

The wonderfully genial irish landlord of this busy old favourite continues to be much in evidence, delightedly mixing with customers as he threads his way though the cheery bustle. It always seems jolly and lively (with quite an overspill outside), but they really go to town around Christmas, Hallowe'en, St Patrick's Day and Churchill's birthday (30 November), when you'll find special events and decorations, and more people than you'd ever imagine could feasibly fit inside. One of the landlord's hobbies is collecting butterflies, so you'll see a variety of prints and books on the subject dotted around the bar. There are also countless lamps, miners' lights, horse tack, bedpans and brasses hanging from the ceiling, a couple of interesting carved figures and statuettes behind the central bar counter, prints of american presidents, and lots of Churchill memorabilia. Well kept Fullers Chiswick, ESB, London Pride and seasonal beers on handpump, with a good choice of wines. The pub can get crowded in the evenings – even early in the week it's not really a place for a quiet pint; it can get a bit smoky too. The spacious and rather smart plant-filled dining conservatory may be used for hatching butterflies, but is better known for its big choice of excellent authentic thai food, such as a very good, proper thai curry, or duck with noodles (all around £5.85); it's no smoking in here. They now do food all day, with other choices including lunchtime sandwiches (from £2.50), ploughman's (£2.50), and Sunday lunch. Fruit machine, TV; they have their own cricket and football teams. *Bar food (12-9.30(4 Sun)) ~ Restaurant ~ (020) 7727 4242 ~ Children in restaurant ~ Dogs welcome ~ Open 11-11; 12-10.30 Sun*

266. WINDSOR CASTLE

Campden Hill Road, W8; ⊖ Holland Park or Notting Hill Gate

One of the delights of this atmospheric Victorian pub is the big tree-shaped garden behind. There are lots of chunky teak seats and tables on flagstones (you'll have to move fast to bag one on a sunny day), as well as a brick outside bar, and quite a secluded feel thanks to the high ivy-covered sheltering walls. While that's a huge draw in summer, this is very much a pub with year-round appeal: the inside is particularly cosy in winter, with its time-smoked ceilings and dark wooden furnishings. The series of tiny unspoilt rooms all have to be entered through separate doors, so it can be quite a challenge finding the people you've arranged to meet – more often than not they'll be hidden behind the high backs of the sturdy built-in elm benches. A cosy pre-war-style dining room opens off, and soft lighting and a coal-effect fire add to the appeal. Served all day, bar food includes things like sandwiches (from

£4.95), steamed mussels or fish and chips (£7.95), and various sausages with mash and onion gravy (£9); they do a choice of roasts on Sunday (£9.95), when the range of other dishes is more limited. Adnams, Fullers London Pride and a guest like Hook Norton on handpump (not cheap, even for this part of London), along with decent house wines, various malt whiskies, and perhaps mulled wine in winter. No fruit machines or piped music. Usually fairly quiet at lunchtime – when several areas are no smoking – the pub can be packed some evenings, often with (as they think) Notting Hill's finest. *Bar food (12-10) ~ (020) 7243 9551 ~ Dogs allowed in bar ~ Open 12-11(10.30 Sun)*

267. BRITANNIA
Allen St; ⊖ High Street Kensington
Friendly civilised local opened into single L-shaped bar, relaxed and peaceful, with good value fresh home-cooked lunches, well kept Youngs and no music; attractive indoor back 'garden' (no smoking at lunchtime); open all day

268. SCARSDALE ARMS
Edwardes Sq; ⊖ High Street Kensington
Busy Georgian pub in lovely leafy square, keeping a good deal of character, with stripped wooden floors, two or three fireplaces with good coal-effect gas fires, lots of knick-knacks, ornate bar counter; well kept ales such as Fullers London Pride, good wine choice, enjoyable blackboard food inc unusual dishes, pleasant service; tree-shaded front courtyard with impressive show of flower tubs and baskets; open all day

W11 (Notting Hill)

269. PORTOBELLO GOLD
Portobello Road, W11; ⊖ Notting Hill Gate

An enjoyable combination of pub, restaurant, hotel and even Internet café, this enterprising place has a cheerfully laid-back, almost bohemian atmosphere. Our favourite part is the rather exotic-seeming back dining room, with a profusion of enormous tropical plants (some up to 25 years old); comfortable wicker chairs, stained wooden tables, and a cage of vocal canaries add to the outdoor effect. The big mural has been replaced with an impressive wall-to-wall mirror. In the old days – when we remember this being a Hell's Angels' hangout – this was the pub garden, and in summer they still open up the sliding roof. The walls here and in the smaller, brightly painted front bar are covered with changing displays of art and photography; the bar also has a nice old fireplace, cushioned pews, daily papers and, more unusually, several Internet terminals (some of which disappear in the evening). The Gold was the first place in the UK to serve oyster shooters (a shot glass with an oyster, parmesan, horseradish, crushed chillies, Tabasco and lime), and they still have something of an emphasis on oysters and seafood; the salt and pepper sits appealingly in oyster shells. There's an almost bewildering number of menus, with good, thoughtfully prepared meals and snacks available all day: you might typically find big toasted ciabattas (from £4.85), soup (£3.95), cajun jumbo shrimp (from £4.95), half a dozen irish rock oysters (£6.95), mexican fajitas or sausage and parsley mash with red onion and tomato gravy (£7.55), fish and chips or lamb cutlets in cumberland sauce (£9.95), and seafood and pasta specials; the puddings come in two sizes. They do good set menus – at lunchtime offering two courses for £10 and three for £13, and in the evenings, two rather more elaborate courses for £14.50, and three for £19. On Sunday, roasts are served until 8pm. You can eat from the same menu in the bar or dining room (part of which is no smoking). Opening at 10 for coffee and fresh pastries, the bar has well kept Brakspears and Shepherd Neame Spitfire, as well as a couple of draught belgian beers, Thatcher's farm cider, a good selection of bottled beers from around the world, and a wide range of interesting tequilas and other well sourced spirits; the wine list is particularly good (the landlady has written books on matching wine with food), and has around a dozen available by the glass. They also have a cigar menu and various coffees. Polite, helpful young staff; piped music, TV (used only for cricket), chess, backgammon. The landlord has compiled a database of what's sold in each of the surrounding antique shops, for those who'd like their browsing slightly more focused. There are one or two tables and chairs on the pretty street outside, which, like the pub, is named in recognition of the 1769 Battle of Portobello, fought over control of the lucrative gold route to Panama. A lively stall is set up outside during the Notting Hill Carnival. Parking

nearby is restricted; it's not always easy to bag a space.
We've yet to hear from people who have stayed overnight
here; the bedrooms all have free Internet access.

*Bar food (12-11(8 Sun)) ~ Restaurant ~ (020) 7460 4910 ~
Children in eating area of bar and restaurant till sundown ~
Dogs allowed in bar ~ Open 10-12; 12-10.30 Sun;
cl 25-31 Dec ~ Bedrooms: £30(£75S)/£45(£85S)*

270. LADBROKE ARMS
Ladbroke Rd; ⊖ Holland Park

Good food on big plates, especially pasta, in smartly chatty dining
pub, Fullers London Pride and Greene King Ruddles County; tables
on front terrace

W14 (West Kensington)

271. COLTON ARMS
Greyhound Road, W14; ⊖ Barons Court

Like a country pub in town, this genuinely old-fashioned little
gem is very much a family concern, kept exactly the same
by its dedicated landlord for the last 30 years. The main
U-shaped front bar has a log fire blazing in winter, highly
polished brasses, a fox's mask, hunting crops and plates
decorated with hunting scenes on the walls, and a
remarkable collection of handsomely carved 17th-c oak
furniture. That room is small enough, and the two back rooms

are tiny; each has its own little serving counter, with a bell to ring for service. Well kept Caledonian Deuchars IPA, Fullers London Pride and Shepherd Neame Spitfire on handpump (when you pay, note the old-fashioned brass-bound till); the food is limited to sandwiches (weekday lunchtimes only, from £2.50). Pull the curtain aside for the door out to a charming back terrace with a neat rose arbour. The pub is next to the Queens Club tennis courts and gardens.

Bar food (12-2 Mon-Sat) ~ No credit cards ~
(020) 7385 6956 ~ Dogs welcome ~ Open 12-3, 5.30-11;
12-4, 7-11(10.30 Sun) Sat

272. HAVELOCK TAVERN

Masbro Road, W14; ⊖ Kensington Olympia

Very classy food is the hallmark of this otherwise ordinary-looking blue-tiled corner house, in an unassuming residential street. Changing every day, the menu might include things like white bean, vegetable and bacon soup with pesto (£4), pork, duck, leek and chorizo terrine (£6), smoked salmon with soft flour tortillas, avocado salsa, coriander and lime (£7.50), asparagus, spring onion and mint omelette or grilled fillets of mackerel with warm bacon, new potato and shallot salad (£8), grilled pork sausages with bubble and squeak and mustard and green peppercorn sauce (£9), pan-fried john dory with sweet and sour red pepper and fennel salad (£10.50), and some unusual cheeses served with apple chutney (£5); you can't book tables. Until 1932 the building was two separate shops (one was a wine merchant, but no one can remember much about the other), and it still has huge shop-front windows along both street-facing walls. The L-shaped bar is plain and unfussy: bare boards, long wooden tables, a mix of chairs and stools, a few soft spotlights, and a fireplace; a second little room with pews leads to a small paved terrace, with benches, a tree, and wall climbers. Well kept (though not cheap) Brakspears, Fullers London Pride and Marstons Pedigree on handpump from the elegant modern bar counter, and a good range of well chosen wines, with around ten by the glass; mulled wine in winter, and in May and June perhaps home-made elderflower soda. Service is friendly and attentive, and the atmosphere relaxed and easy-going; no music or machines, but plenty of chat from the varied range of customers – at busy times it can seem really quite noisy. Backgammon, chess, Scrabble and other board games. Though evenings are always busy (you may have to wait for a table then, and some dishes can run out quite quickly), it can be quieter at lunchtimes, and in the afternoons can have something of the feel of a civilised private club. On weekdays, parking nearby is metered.

Bar food (12.30-2.30, 7-10) ~ No credit cards ~
(020) 7603 5374 ~ Children welcome ~ Dogs welcome ~
Open 11-11; 12-10.30 Sun; cl second Mon in Aug, 22-26
Dec

273. BEACONSFIELD
Blythe Rd; ⊖ Kensington Olympia
Open-plan former Frigate & Firkin reworked with pastel café-bar décor; three well kept real ales and Inch's farm cider, friendly staff, lunchtime food; games machine, big-screen TV; pavement picnic-sets; open all day

274. WARWICK ARMS
Warwick Rd; ⊖ Kensington Olympia
Early 19th-c, with lots of old woodwork, comfortable atmosphere, friendly regulars (some playing darts or bridge), good service; well kept Fullers beers from elegant Wedgwood handpumps, limited tasty food (not Sun evening), sensible prices, no piped music; open all day; tables outside, handy for Earls Court and Olympia

EAST LONDON

275. KICK

Shoreditch High Street, E1; ⊖ Old Street

Homely and relaxed, with the convivial atmosphere of a continental games café, this compact place has four working table-footer tables, with more hung on the walls alongside other appropriate memorabilia including a giant footer-player figurehead, and virtually continuous tournaments and leagues not entirely monopolised by the 20-somethings. The ceiling is draped with flags and, besides the Formica chairs and tables (all with fresh flowers) on the bare boards, one cherished alcove has three soft leather settees around a low table. The cheerfully staffed bar is strong on foreign bottled beers and spirits (especially rums and tequilas), with cut-price cocktails in the late afternoon and early evening, and good coffees and hot chocolate. An open kitchen at the back serves food such as marinated olives (£2.50), garlic mushrooms or chorizo in wine (£3.50), enterprising sandwiches such as chorizo with rocket (£5) or serrano ham with manchego cheese (£5.50), smoked mackerel and avocado salad (£5.50), toulouse sausage and mash with home-made onion confit (£7.50), and organic pork and apple stew (£8.50). They have daily papers, a vintage bagatelle machine, well reproduced piped music, a couple of plasma TVs, and plenty of local posters; a basement bar with more up-to-date

furnishings is opened at busy times. There are pavement tables out by the busy road.
Bar food (12-3.30, 6-11; all day Sat and Sun) ~ (020) 7739 8700 ~ Children at lunchtime only ~ Open 12-11(12 Thurs-Sat, 10.30 Sun); closed 24-26 Dec, 1 Jan

276. PROSPECT OF WHITBY
Wapping Wall, E1; ⊖ Wapping

The view of the Thames from this entertaining old pub can hardly be bettered, and has been a draw since it was a favourite with smugglers and river thieves, back when the pub was known as the Devil's Tavern. It has such a lively history it's no wonder they do rather play on it; the tourists who flock here lap up the colourful tales of Merrie Olde London, and only the most unromantic of visitors could fail to be carried along by the fun. Pepys and Dickens were both frequent callers, Turner came for weeks at a time to study its river views, and in the 17th c the notorious Hanging Judge Jeffreys was able to combine two of his interests by enjoying a drink at the back while looking down over the grisly goings-on in Execution Dock. The pub is an established favourite with evening coach tours, but is usually quieter at lunchtimes. Plenty of bare beams, bare boards, panelling and flagstones in the L-shaped bar (where the long pewter counter is over 400 years old), and a river view towards Docklands from tables in the waterfront courtyard. Well kept Adnams, Courage Directors, Fullers London Pride and

Greene King Old Speckled Hen on handpump, and quite a few malt whiskies. Bar meals are served all day, from a menu including sandwiches and filled baked potatoes (from £3.25), various burgers (from £4.95), ploughman's (£5.25), roasted red pepper lasagne (£7.75), and jamaican jerk spiced chicken (£9.75). One area of the bar is no smoking; fruit machine, golf game.

Bar food (12-9) ~ Restaurant ~ (020) 7481 1095 ~ Children welcome ~ Dogs allowed in bar ~ Open 11.30-11; 12-10.30 Sun

277. CAPTAIN KIDD
Wapping High St; ⊖ Wapping
Thames views from large, open-plan, nautical-theme pub's jutting bay windows, in renovated Docklands warehouse stripped back to beams and basics; good choice of hot and cold food all day inc several puddings, Sam Smiths keg beers, obliging bow-tied staff, lively bustle; sports TV; chunky tables on roomy back waterside terrace

278. DICKENS INN
Marble Quay, St Katharines Way; ⊖ Tower Hill
Outstanding position above smart Docklands marina, oddly swiss-chalet look from outside with its balconies and window boxes, interesting stripped-down bare boards, baulks and timbers interior; wide choice of enjoyable food, well kept Theakstons Old Peculier, friendly prompt service, several floors inc big pricy restaurant extension; popular with overseas visitors, seats outside

279. GOLDEN HEART
Commercial St; ⊖ Shoreditch
Warmly welcoming landlady, good informal atmosphere; popular with what might be called the Turner Prize school of artists

280. GOOD SAMARITAN
Turner St/Stepney Way; ⊖ Whitechapel
Spick-and-span well run pub, reasonably priced food, cheerful prompt service, Courage Directors and Theakstons from central bar; Victorian photographs

281. VIBE BAR
Truman Building, Brick Lane; ⊖ Shoreditch
In part of an old brewery, and buzzing in summer when the large cobbled courtyard with trees and wooden picnic-sets has a bar and indian food servery; through a purple corridor, the big very dimly lit square bar has comfortable, well spaced red and brown button-back leather settees, padded benches, and a couple of sets of elegant wrought-iron dining tables and chairs; amber candle-holders on battered tables, twisty pink, red and white spotlights, bare boards and brickwork, and graffiti all over one wall; lagers on tap, free Internet access, laid-back staff, and emphasis on the innovative music, with popular DJ and live music nights; some seating too in a glass-roofed terrace area

E2 (Bethnal Green)

282. APPROACH TAVERN
Approach Road, E2; ⊖ Bethnal Green
This imposing high-ceilinged Victorian tavern, handy for the Museum of Childhood on Bethnal Green, has been restored

as an easy-going food pub. What they serve is good and gently inventive without being pretentious – soup (£4), ciabattas (£4.50), pork and leek sausages with mustard mash and gravy or butternut squash and field mushroom risotto (£8), beer-battered cod and chips (£8.50), chicken breast roasted with chorizo (£9), delicious puddings (£3.50), and popular Sunday roasts – even the nut roast comes in for praise here. The big-windowed main bar is thoroughly traditional, with sturdy old-fashioned wall settles, studded dark leatherette carvers and pews (some carved) around heavy pub tables on bare boards, lamps hanging from the high ochre Anaglypta ceiling, and some interesting photographs; there is more seating in a back room with a dark green décor. Well kept Fullers London Pride and Ridleys IPA, Prospect and Old Bob on handpump, continental beers on tap, daily papers, considerate service from the swedish landlady and her staff – and an amiable mix of customers that reflect the largely but not entirely fashionable face of new young Hackney. The non-contemporary jukebox has an outstanding choice, and there may be a handsome flower arrangement on the mantelpiece in front of the large mirror. Upstairs is an art gallery. The railed and heated front terrace, fairy-lit at night, has tables shaded by plane trees.
Bar food (12-2.30(3 Sat), 6-9.30; 12-4 Sun, not Sun evening) ~ (020) 8980 2321 ~ Children welcome ~ Open 12-11(10.30 Sun); cl 26 Dec

E3 (Hackney/Bow)

283. CROWN

Grove Road/Old Ford Road, E3; ⊖ Mile End

On quite a busy roundabout facing Victoria Park with its popular boating lake, this idiosyncratic pub is notable for its organic food and drinks, and its proudly recycled furnishings. Despite the big windows, it's dim inside, thanks to the very dark ceiling, some dark brown walls, and soft lighting (evidently powered by solar or wind generation) from lamps that include some big retirees from a hospital operating theatre. There is an easy-going jumble of mainly stripped tables in all sorts of sizes on the dark floorboards, with a similar mix of chairs; a couple of corners have well worn easy chairs, and big abstracts decorate the walls. Good freshly cooked food makes its entrance down broad stairs below a crystal chandelier; the big blackboard might include spinach and parsley soup (£3), cumberland sausage and chutney (£4.50), smoked mackerel pâté with pickled cucumber and toast (£7), cured salmon with lemon, vodka and pepper or full english brunch (£8.50), butternut squash and chestnut risotto (£9.50), and rib-eye steak with root vegetable chips (£14.50), with puddings such as chocolate, prune and armagnac terrine (£5); bar snacks are available all day, and they do children's helpings. They have a fine choice of organic wines and other drinks, including on handpump the all-organic local Pitfield beers (one named for

the pub's hands-on joint owner Geetie Singh) and St Peters
Organic Best real ales. The relaxed mix of customers may
include the odd friendly dog, and there are some pleasant
courtyard tables.
*Bar food (12-4 (not Mon), 6.30–10.30; 10.30-4,
6.30-10.30 Sat and Sun) ~ (020) 8981 9998 ~ Children
welcome ~ Dogs allowed in bar ~ Open
12(10.30 Sat and Sun)-11; cl till 5pm Mon, all 25 Dec*

284. PALM TREE
Haverfield Rd; ⊖ Mile End
Lone survivor of blitzed East End terrace, by Regent's Canal and
beside windmill and ecology centre in futuristic-looking Mile End
Park; horseshoe bar, many original features, thriving local
atmosphere

E4 (Chingford)

285. PLOUGH
Mott St/Sewardstone Rd (A112); no nearby station
McMullens pub with beamery and concrete paving, their beers kept
well, good choice of decent food; picnic-sets outside with attractive
flowers and tubs

E11 (Snaresbrook)

286. DUKE OF EDINBURGH
Nightingale Lane; ⊖ Snaresbrook
Comfortably unspoilt two-bar local, warm and friendly, with good
plain cheap lunchtime food (all home-made), well kept Adnams and

guest beers, decent wine, cheerful service; plenty of prints and plates, even an aquarium; garden tables; open all day

E12 (East Ham)

287. RUSKIN ARMS
High St North; ⊖ East Ham
Local with big back music room – live bands Fri, DJs Sat

E14 (Limehouse/Stepney)

288. GRAPES
Narrow Street, E14; ⊖ Shadwell (some distance away) or Westferry on the DLR; the Limehouse link has made it hard to find by car – turn off Commercial Road at signs for Rotherhithe Tunnel, then from the Tunnel Approach slip road, fork left leading into Branch Road, turn left and then left again into Narrow Street

In a peaceful spot well off the tourist route, this warmly welcoming 16th-c tavern is one of London's most engaging riverside pubs. It was used by Charles Dickens as the basis of his Six Jolly Fellowship Porters in *Our Mutual Friend*, and little has changed since he prophetically wrote 'It had not a straight floor and hardly a straight line, but it had outlasted and would yet outlast many a better-trimmed building, many a sprucer public house'. The back part is the oldest, with the

small back balcony a fine place for a sheltered waterside drink; steps lead down to the foreshore. The partly panelled bar has lots of prints, mainly of actors, some elaborately etched windows, and newspapers to read. Well kept Adnams, Bass and Ind Coope Burton on handpump, a choice of malt whiskies, and a good wine list. Good bar food includes soup (£2.95), sandwiches (from £3.25), bangers and mash (£5.75), home-made fishcakes with caper sauce (£5.95), dressed crab (£7.25), and a highly regarded, generous roast on Sunday (no other meals then, when it can be busy, particularly in season). They do an excellent brunch on Saturday lunchtimes. Booking is recommended for the upstairs fish restaurant, which has fine views of the river (the pub was a favourite with Rex Whistler, who used it as the viewpoint for his rather special river paintings). Shove-ha'penny, table skittles, cribbage, dominoes, chess, backgammon; there may be piped classical music or jazz.
Bar food (not Sun evening) ~ Restaurant ~ (020) 7987 4396 ~ Dogs allowed in bar ~ Open 12-3, 5.30-11; 12-11 Sat; 12-10.30 Sun; closed 25-26 Dec, 1 Jan

289. BARLEY MOW
Narrow St; Limehouse DLR
Steep steps down into converted dockmaster's house, clean and comfortable, with Victorian-style wallpaper over dark panelled dado, lots of sepia Whitby photographs, candles and ships' lanterns; reasonably priced usual food from sandwiches up, well kept ales such as Greene King IPA, partly panelled conservatory with stained-glass

french windows; big heaters for picnic-sets on spacious if breezy terrace with great views over two Thames reaches; swing-bridge entrance to Limehouse Basin and mouth of Regent's Canal still has electric windlass used for hauling barges through; children and dogs welcome, car park with CCTV

290. GEORGE
Glengall Grove; Crossharbour & London Arena DLR
Cheery East End pub with Courage Best and Greene King Ruddles, good food inc bargain specials and market-fresh fish; bar (Isle of Dogs old guard), lounge (new City types) and conservatory dining room

E17 (Walthamstow)

291. FLOWER POT
Wood St; ⇌ Wood Street
Friendly single bar with good atmosphere and particularly well kept Bass and Charles Wells Bombardier; popular with soccer fans

TEN TOP HOTEL BARS

The editor of this *Guide* still smarts from the day many years ago when, on his only attempt ever to eat in the Savoy Hotel, he turned up for a birthday meal proudly kitted out in an italian leather jacket which had cost him well over a week's wages, only to be barred by a sniffy waiter who turned his nose up at it as 'Something which would suit, shall we say, a lorry driver'.

How times have changed. In a round of anonymous inspections for this book, we found that even the grandest hotel bars were welcoming to all, however casually dressed. Though we saw nobody looking decidedly scruffy, men wearing ties were usually outnumbered by those who were not. Yes, the surroundings are smart – some are very smart indeed – but the atmosphere is pleasantly informal and relaxed.

These top hotel bars are an interesting and stylish alternative to more obvious drinking places – at a price. Reckon on paying two or three times as much as in a pub. The multiple seems greatest at the bottom of the price scale (for a basic soft drink, say), easing as you go up the quality/complexity scale.

What you get for your money is a level of unhurried comfort and 'specialness' which ordinary bars and pubs can't match.

At the bigger places especially, the choice of wines by the glass is superb, and cocktails come not from some plastic list but from a long tradition of real expertise (many of the classics were invented in these bars, in particular the Savoy). All will rustle up at least something to eat at any time of day (in the individual reports we mention only unusual specialities), not to mention tea or coffee – tea service can be quite an impressive production. All can produce and advise on properly kept Havana cigars (again, the bigger places have a fine choice), yet we did not find any of the bars to be smoky. Beyond the bars we describe, there is usually a range of other places (often including secondary bars as well as extensive comfortable lounges) where you can sit with a drink instead. Service is normally impeccable, and far-reaching (heavy shopping bags or coats will be looked after for you, if you want). And you are much more likely to spot famous faces.

So next time you feel like splashing out on a special occasion, give one of the great hotel bars a try.

Children are in general not banned from these hotel bars, but in each case there is no doubt that families with young children would feel a lot more comfortable in one of the hotel's other public rooms.

It is worth bearing in mind some major differences from more run-of-the-mill watering holes:

• Though there may be a few bar stools, drinks are brought to your table

- Don't expect to find real ale (we didn't notice a single handpump)
- Do expect a generous supply of good free nibbles – usually a set of three bowls, perhaps with hand-cut kettle-fried potato and vegetable crisps, top-grade nuts such as cashews, macadamias and shelled pistachios, and giant olives or savoury bakes
- Ten minutes before you want to leave, get your bill – this normally comes in a fat leather book on a salver, and the whole process can easily take that long
- Enjoy the lavatories – a particular highlight, with superb service, at the Connaught, memorable too at the Savoy, Claridge's and the Ritz.

The one disappointment is that piped music does tend to crop up even in some of the best of these bars – it does rather lower the tone.

BROWNS

33 Albemarle Street, W1

From entrance turn right, going along extensive lounge (very popular for tea and coffee), to bar at end; but NB: Browns will be closed for much of 2004 for major refurbishment, so the layout may change

A nice burble of relaxed chatter fills this popular interior bar in the heart of Mayfair; men and women meeting from work, mixed with residents, often from across the Atlantic. Horn-coloured leather bucket chairs, some big brocaded wing armchairs and navy leather settees are grouped around mahogany tripod tables and roll-end ones (looking like elevated piano stools); the moulded panelling has small misty lithographs and gilt lamps, and there is an imposing fireplace. Two or three barmen in red waistcoats work the mirror-backed bar, which does have a row of bar stools. There is a fine choice of wines by the glass and other drinks; nibbles are good. On our visit, very faint piped music featured jazz singers such as Ella Fitzgerald.

CAPITAL

22–24 Basil Street, SW3

Bar on right just past reception

This small interior bar faces the hotel's good stylish restaurant, and is used by many of the restaurant customers (including regular local business lunchers), as well as quietly chatting hotel residents. Black-bow-tied formally dressed staff are much in evidence, and you may be greeted two or three times on your way in. The proper serving bar, with bar stools in use, has an excellent choice of wines by the glass and other drinks. Low gilt tables with green-and-gold glass tops, like polished moss agate, have comfortable chairs and attractively patterned banquettes set into bleached carved panelling inset with elaborately cut and etched mirrors. Add in the soft lighting, a big pot of flowering orchids, and another of coloured willow wands, and the effect is of carefully designed luxury not unlike those advertisements of elaborate interiors in *Country Life*. This is a relaxing retreat from the bustle of Harrods, just around the corner, and just a short stroll from Sloane Street.

CHESTERFIELD
35 Charles Street, W1
Bar on right of reception

Unusual in tabling a bar food menu with a whole range of rather pubby food (including sandwiches, from £6.25 up), and in its daytime piped music (again, along the lines of what you might hear in many pubs), this interior bar strikes a nice balance between friendly informality and all the trimmings of a serious hotel bar. The choice of wines (and champagnes) by the glass is not so wide as in some, but is thoughtful and rewarding (there are plenty of other drinks to consider) nibbles are good and unusual, they have a rack of daily papers, and friendly white-jacketed bar service is nicely old-fashioned. Antique engravings of Lord Chesterfield (the 4th Earl, 18th-c statesman and wit) and his circle and connections line the deep green walls three-deep. He would appreciate the irony of figuring as mascot for a bar; in one of his celebrated letters to his son (27 March, 1747) he wrote, 'I always naturally hated drinking; and yet I have often drunk, with disgust at the time, attended by great sickness the next day, only because I then considered drinking as a necessary qualification for a fine Gentleman, and a Man of Pleasure. Thus seduced by fashion, and blindly adopting nominal ones, I lost real pleasures.' The green motif runs right through the décor, which includes potted palms; the choicest seats are a pair of great tapestried banquettes covered with scatter cushions, in a side alcove, though the bar stools (below a row of staffordshire dogs) are perfectly comfortable. A pianist performs every night except Sunday.

CLARIDGE'S
Brook Street, W1
Bar signed on right of main entrance; those in the know, instead, use the unmarked door on Davies Street, closest to the corner with Brook Street, which leads straight in

Surprisingly unstuffy, this, with plenty of neat, pleasant staff. Three linked rooms have the serving bar at one end – on our visit, its coffee machine cheerfully letting off steam, piped Ella Fitzgerald, and one or two women busy on their mobile phones, added to an unexpected feeling of informal bustle. Our fellow-customers included both locals (well known art and antiques dealers among them, chatting over cigars and champagne) and foreign visitors, particularly from across the Atlantic (tea in graceful serving sets seemed their favoured tipple). The restrained décor gives a slightly colonnaded stone-faced appearance to the two rooms nearest the serving bar, which has extremely comfortable bar stools. There are small curved red leather banquettes and classical small armchairs on the wood strip floor, with a nicely lit paphiopedilum orchid in full flower in a glazed-over deco fireplace. The further room, with softer lighting and a darker décor, is more intimate. Drinks and bar nibbles (served here in elegant modernist china sets of four rather than the silver-plate triplets so pervasive elsewhere) are first class.

CONNAUGHT
16 Carlos Place, W1
Main bar on right of entrance hall

This lovely, beautifully proportioned room houses perhaps the most civilised of all London's great hotel bars. Only the very occasional mobile phone user reminds you that you are in cosmopolitan London, rather than a peaceful country house hotel. Two big fireplaces, each with a large matching mirror above, face each other down the length of the room, with its handsome carpet woven to fit, elaborate ceiling plasterwork, tall luxuriously curtained windows, comfortable armchairs and curvy corner settees. Gun-room paintings decorate the discreetly moulded panelling, a bracket clock ticks steadily between silver candelabra, and the décor of muted pinks, beiges, buffs and maroons helps the relaxed and restful atmosphere. A heavy mahogany bar counter has clubby leather bar stools, and service is excellent – neatly unobtrusive, and not too formal. Besides the unimpeachable drinks choice, they serve interesting tapas (three for £10). The courtly cloakroom service is superb.

DURRANTS
26–32 George Street, W1
Bar has own entrance, with restaurant, to left of main hotel entrance

Handy for Oxford Street and Baker Street, this appealing little bar has nothing of the grand hotel about it. Durrants is a long and attractive Georgian building, run by the same family for many years, and the bar is a friendly home-from-home for tweedy gents up from Devon or Yorkshire. It has old leather banquettes, deep mahogany bucket chairs and a couple of wing armchairs around just five or six small tables that look like copper-topped bar stools. Our visit on a windy but very mild autumn day found stray gusts bringing one or two fallen leaves swirling past the window boxes and in at one of the two antique sash windows; it made a refreshing difference from the air conditioning of bigger places. Sporting oil paintings, antique handguns and a mercury barometer adorn the old pine panelling, there is a little black-leaded fireplace, and a welcoming white-jacketed barman presides over the small bar counter, which has four bar stools: like stepping back several decades. Drinks choice, and nibbles, are not on such a grand scale as in the bigger hotels, but are good, and service is very good. A very likeable place.

LANESBOROUGH
Lanesborough Place, SW1
Library bar on left of entrance hall

Right on Hyde Park Corner, this imposing building with its colonnaded portico used to be the Middlesex Hospital, and has recently been converted, at obvious expense, to a luxury hotel. The comfortable bar has tall ceilings, massive dark mahogany panelling and glass-fronted bookcases serving to display bottles and cigars as well as some leathery books, country-house settees, figured walnut glass-topped tables and big chinese rugs on polished pale oak parquet, heavy drapes as well as net curtains for the tall windows (no traffic noise seeps through), candelabra and a huge Reynolds-look portrait above the marble fireplace (with a flame-effect fire);

also, cut-crystal glasses and Royal Worcester bramble-pattern porcelain dishes and ashtrays. Given this aura of heavy opulence, it was something of a surprise to hear not only piped music but also staff conducting lengthy trade telephone calls in full view; but at least the music was Dave Brubeck and the like, and some might find those phone calls add a pleasantly downbeat human touch. Hyde Park is over the road, and Buckingham Palace is just down Constitution Hill.

ONE ALDWYCH

1 Aldwych, WC2
Lobby bar on left of main entrance

This is the most modern in style of our collection of top hotel bars, with a striking centrepiece in the form of an over-life-size expressionist bronze figure of an oarsman afloat among the well spaced lacquered coffee tables. Tall arched windows set shadows from the sunlit plane trees outside dancing on the broad white rubberised flooring tiles. Besides comfortable buff-upholstered bucket seats and a few small settees, some immensely high-backed, faintly pharaonic, chairs call to mind the nearby Royal Opera House's recent production of *Aida*, and geometric patterned rugs set into the floor add a touch of muted colour. The whole effect is light, airy and up-to-date, with rather bright and lively acoustics, plenty of obliging staff, and a busy coffee machine hissing away at the well stocked bar which forms the apex of this triangular lofty-ceilinged room. An extensive choice of wines by the glass includes several champagnes, and in the evenings they do some interesting bar food such as eight baby sausages (£7.65), half a dozen smoked salmon canapés (£8.50), and fish sushi (£12.95).

RITZ
150 Piccadilly, W1 (entrance now round corner in Arlington Street)
Head straight down into main concourse and Rivoli bar is on your right

The most lushly exotic of the top bars, this is art deco with none of the restraint that normally moderates that style. Backlit Lalique nudes, stylised mirrored murals and a big relief of Leda and the Swan are set into gilt-belted walls that look like tortoiseshell; orchids spill out of internally lit alabaster columns and urns, and arched and gilded embrasures hold rich flower arrangements; fanciful curly sculptures of light (no mere light fittings these) ornament the low ceiling. Around beautiful tables of what looks like butter-coloured onyx are comfortable gilt chairs and settees in heavy brocade or a leopard-skin print. A young cream-jacketed team mans the busy smallish counter (which has comfortable bar stools), and the choice of drinks – served with the style you'd expect from the surroundings – seems limitless; the nibbles are very good. As the bar has no windows and is not large (there is plenty of seating space out in the airy concourse), it has a pleasantly intimate feel, and a nice mix of users from some local people through out-of-town visitors to those from overseas. On our visit, there was enough contented chatter to veil the very faint background of piped hotel music.

SAVOY

1 Savoy Hill, WC2 (main entrance is from front courtyard, off the Strand at around number 93)
American bar up broad steps on left of main entrance lobby

An impressive monument to 1920-30s art deco, this bar though spacious feels intimate and relaxed. Divided into two main areas, it has cosy corners and alcoves; gentle curves and rounded wall ends go well with the expansive feel you get as you stroll over the handsomely deco-patterned dark blue carpet, to sink into one of the comfortable dark blue or gold seats around the brass-bound black-lacquered tables. The cream walls have a fine collection of silver-framed theatrical photographs, and the small end bar counter (with two or three rather splendid bar stools) somehow conjures up cinema images – perhaps because of the screen-shaped mirrored back. Though there are some windows in the part by the bar counter (you can catch a glimpse of the Thames), this is best thought of as an interior bar. Service is splendidly discreet and unobtrusive; much of the work is done off-stage in what must be an absolute powerhouse of drinks-making, so vast is the choice available to you. Drinks come with excellent nibbles. The Savoy's cocktails are legendary, and the original *Savoy Cocktail Book* (1930) is still a much-reprinted standard work – our own favourite is a Jack Rose made with lime not lemon. You may see politicians and power-brokers here, but there's a pleasantly broad mix including casually dressed media deal-makers (with their mobile phones, alas), youngish couples, women chatting and so forth. Good acoustics make it easy to have very private conversations here.

MAPS

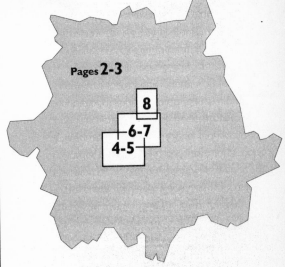

BEST
LONDON
PUBS &
BARS

Pages 2-3

8

6-7

4-5

144 Pub listing number

Pubs are indicated on the maps in their approximate positions only.
If you are unsure of the location of a particular pub, you are strongly
advised to check exactly where it is before setting out.

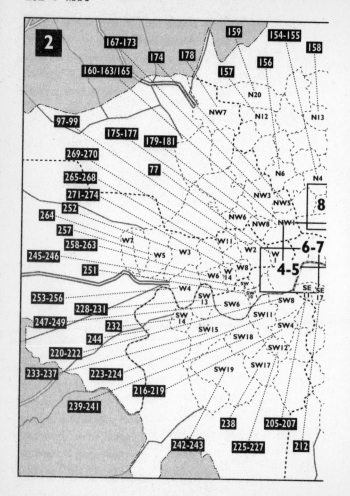

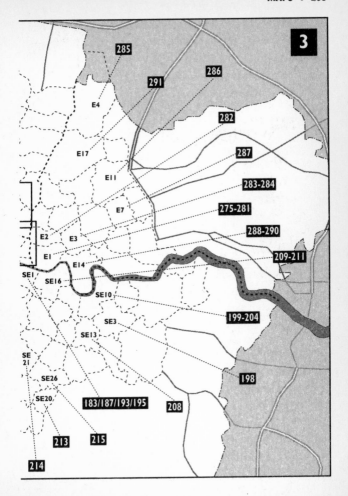

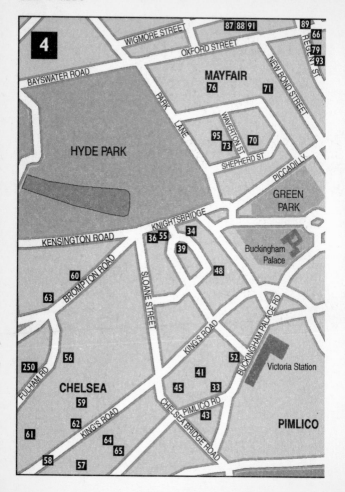

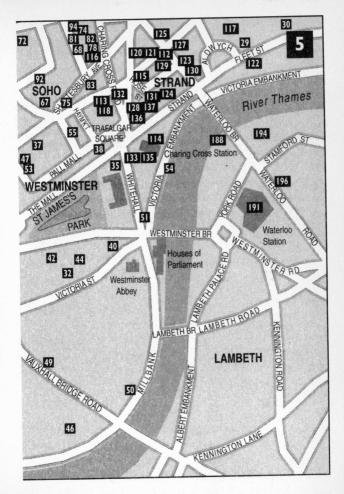

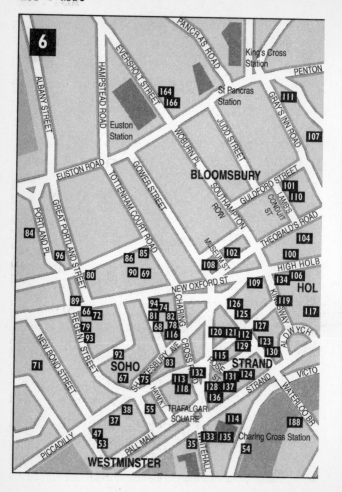

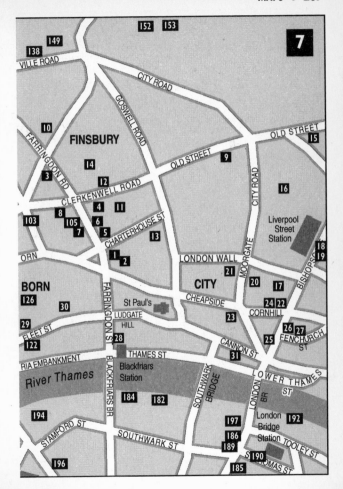

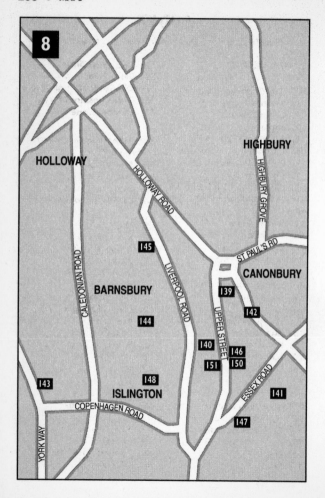

INDEX

Pub listing number   **Pub name**   Page number